The Remarkable Story of John & Anne Gimenez

upon this ROCK

The Miracle of Rock Church

as told to Robert Paul Lamb

Souls Books
1815 12th Avenue
Columbus, GA 31901

Unless otherwise identified, Scripture quotations are from the King James
Version of the Bible.

Library of Congress Number: 79-67430

First Edition — October 1979

Contents

Preface

Foreward

1   Free at Last   11

2   The Newlyweds   21

3   An Answer to Prayer   35

4   "I Know Where There's An Empty Church Building ..."   41

5   3101 Lens Avenue   55

6   Trials, Tests and Temptations   61

7   "Are You Ashamed of Me?"   67

8   Divine Intervention   77

9   "Arise and Build"   83

10   Following The Spirit's Bidding   107

11   The Pillar of Cloud Moves   121

12   "The Witch of Kempsville"   133

13   Raising Up The Staff   147

14   The Round Building   155

15   Hitting the Airwaves   165

16   "When Is Rock Church Gonna Quit Growing?"   173

TO:
The people of Rock Church

"... and upon this rock I will build my church; and the gates of hell shall not prevail against it."
—Matthew 16:18

Preface

The story of how this book came to be written is a marvel to me. In March 1979, I attended a leadership conference at Ridgecrest Baptist Center outside Montreat, N.C. John Gimenez had flown there to announce plans for the "Washington for Jesus" rally.

At breakfast one morning, I saw two friends eating together and decided to join them. Within a few minutes, John, who I'd never met but who knew both men, appeared, a breakfast tray in hand.

Finding out that John was a friend of two men I'd done books with — Jim Bakker and Jesse Winley — he and I had much common ground for conversation. He told me about his exciting plans for the Washington rally. It was a completely spontaneous meeting — just two Christian brothers sharing about the Lord and themselves.

In time, the two other men left. Soon, the lunchroom cleared out entirely. John and I were left alone except for a cleaning crew.

"Brother, do you feel the need to pray?" I asked, suddenly feeling an impulse to do so.

"No, but we can," he said.

Taking hands, we launched into prayer. Then, I wondered, "Brother, do you feel like you have a word from the Lord?"

"I don't know," he answered.

Several moments passed. Then, he suddenly began praying loudly in tongues. I could feel the Baptist rafters vibrating. The interpretation followed.

"Surely I have called thee together to do a work for Me that I might be glorified in this day. Write the word which I have placed upon My servant's heart. Write all the words of the Lord. And to the scribe, the Lord will give a fleet pen to work inspiration among His people."

It seemed like a scene right from the pages of the Old Testament between Jeremiah and Baruch. I felt then, even as I do now, that John Gimenez and I kept a divine appointment that day.

Demos Shakarian, as well as many others, had encouraged John to get a book written on his intriguing life. But after some unsuccessful attempts at getting the venture off the ground, John backed away. "Lord, I'll not make another move. I'm waiting on you."

The next day, we met.

This book started out to be *just* John's story. But then, we — John, Anne and myself — discovered the story would only be half told if it were written that way. The book was switched to a third person account to cover Anne's vital part of the ministry.

Without question, their marriage and ministry is one of the most unique around. Anne says they're both extremists "in our own ways." She's probably right. John, a personable, outgoing man, is totally consumed in his work for the Lord. Yet, at the same time, he's constantly looking for new challenges.

In the pulpit, Anne becomes a fiery, finger-pointing evangelist. At heart, though, she is a private person whose main interest is her husband and child. Yet, opposites attract, I believe, making for good marriages and ministries. The Gimenezes have both.

They are both bold as lions in speaking the Word of the Lord, but then gentle as lambs when need be. I clearly see the touch of God within that. Of all the things I appreciate about them, there is one that stands out above the rest. Once they've heard a word from God on a matter, they're completely fearless to follow it. They will not be deterred. In many ways Rock Church is a testimony to that kind of "hearing" and then, obeying.

This book represents a first in several ways. It's the first book for Souls Books. And it's the Gimenez' first book together, although John's earlier story was told in *Up Tight.*

I, as well as John and Anne, owe a huge debt of appreciation for many people who've helped in this project. Three people stand out in particular: John Hathaway, Joe Lust and Dennis Auth — all extremely talented and creative men, who happen to be members of Rock Church.

I am also very grateful to my precious wife, Cynthia, and my two children, Lesley and Lindsey, for allowing me to be away from home so much during the writing of this book. They are a considerable credit to everything I do.

Upon This Rock comes covered in prayer that it might bless, encourage and strengthen every person who reads it. To God be the glory ... great things He hath done.

Robert Paul Lamb

Foreword

In the fourteen years since I first met John Gimenez, I have watched miracle after miracle occur within his and Anne's far-reaching ministry. Their story vividly demonstrates the grace and mercy of God working in the lives of two people who've committed their way unto Jesus Christ.

I first came in touch with John when "The Addicts" presented their gripping drama on drug addiction before the 1965 Full Gospel Businessmen's World Convention in Chicago. As the play was given that night, I sat weeping over the mighty delivering power of God in these young men's lives. The meeting hall was shaken and many lives were transformed.

Subsequently — when God miraculously provided over $3,000 for airfare — John took a team of "Addicts" on a Full Gospel Businessmen's Airlift to England. Through John's efforts, more than a hundred drug addicts from the rugged Soho section of London were converted to Christ. Not a single addict ever showed signs of withdrawal.

The news of the addicts' conversions hit the London newspapers. When six officers from the Scotland Yard drug squad heard about what happened, they came to the convention, were saved and filled with the Holy Spirit. "Jesus Christ is the only thing that could make such a change in those addicts' lives," one officer said. "That convinced us to repent."

In the years since, God has continued to demonstrate His mighty hand upon John and Anne. Rock Church is one of the most outstanding churches that I know about. It's always a great thrill for me to go there. In fact, when I'm on the east coast and away from home in California, I consider Rock Church to be "my church."

It has been such a great joy for me to watch much of this inspiring story unfold. That's why I personally have such confidence in John and Anne Gimenez. No one could have accomplished what they have without the hand of God being upon them. Without question, they are both chosen vessels of the Lord.

I pray that everyone who reads this fascinating book will do so carefully because of the credibility of the Gimenez' lives and the never-changing Bible principles they learned. Inspiration and encouragement live within these pages. This story is true, factual and honest. It really happened.

It is graphic evidence of what God can do through the lives of yielded vessels. That's why I want to personally endorse this book. There is something here for every Christian.

Demos Shakarian

1

Free At Last

A fleeting hour or so was all that remained to the late August afternoon and the once blazing sun slipped leisurely down the red and gold western sky. John Gimenez sat pensively for a long time looking into the deep, narrow valley alternately turning mossy gray and then bright green as bands of striated sunlight broke through fleecy white clouds.

His upstairs room on the third floor held a panoramic view of several rugged mountain ranges in northern Pennsylvania near the New York state line. The house, a rambling but aging wooden structure with peeling white paint and leaking roof, belonged to David Minor, an unusually tender-hearted preacher, who lived on the main floor and conducted church services in the basement.

A tiny dot on the map of Pennsylvania, Coudersport represented the end of the line for John. Already he had spent several weeks there laboring alongside Brother Minor, who besides pastoring, supported himself through assorted carpentry jobs. Nobody else seemingly would take John in except the smiling, tall pastor. His specialty was housing homeless waifs and mending the crippled.

Without question, John Gimenez fit both those categories.

The ministry he'd once known had evaporated. His group, "The Addicts," had disbanded. They had sung and given their testimonies of deliverance from drugs in churches from coast to coast. A movie, "Way Out," had been made about them. John had even told his own hellish story of drug addiction in a book. Acclaim followed.

Soon four teams of "Addicts" hit the road singing, testifying, witnessing and presenting a play John had written. Doors opened everywhere — throughout the states and as far away as London. "The Addicts" were constantly appearing before large conventions and packed churches.

Then, it happened. The delicate thread that held the ministry together snapped and began to unravel. Some of the guys slipped, dabbled in drugs, then backslid. The four travel vans were quickly repossessed. "The Addicts" scattered like confused animals — many of them back to the streets from which they came.

Even though he led "The Addicts," John Gimenez was no different. He too was caught in a powerful undertow, dragged down by his old haunting lifestyle. For a year he struggled through Elim Bible Institute at Lima, New York, causing problems for the faculty and himself. Overcome by old habits and rebellion, John's once-active ministry came to a dead stop. Inwardly he grew cold and isolated from God's Presence.

At times when he looked back, John realized everything had been running smoothly until Anne Nethery had prophesied over him. He remembered the prophecy like it was yesterday.

"The Addicts" had been laboring futilely through a church service without any anointing. John stopped the service and called for prayer. Sensing the problem, the pastor walked back to Anne visiting in the church and asked her to take the service. "If you feel led," he suggested.

A hush fell over the crowd as Anne walked to the front. "I believe the Lord wants us to lift up each one of the guys in prayer," she announced. Then, she and the pastor laid hands on each member of "The Addicts" and Anne prophesied.

When they approached John, she held back hoping the pastor would pray. Several moments passed, then Anne reluctantly placed her hands on him and prophesied.

"I have brought thee forth from a pit and I have put My Spirit in thee," erupted the powerful Word of God, *"but thou hast forsaken Me. Thus, I will strip thee and make thee as one who is naked. But I again shall build thee and what is built will be of Me."*

At the time, the prophecy didn't mean much. John simply grew irritated at Anne for having the gumption to say such things. "This ministry's booming," he thought to himself. "Things couldn't be better." And above all, he surely didn't need some woman preacher telling him any different.

But in a matter of months, the unthinkable happened. The prophecy came true. John Gimenez found himself stripped. He was down to nothing — barely surviving off the helping hand of a sympathetic pas-

tor. Just like many before, he had touched the glory of
God. Once he had become tainted though, the glory
departed.

In some ways John thought to himself, it was best
that Anne had given him such a staggering prophecy.
Who else could have done it and not gotten a broken
jaw in the process? Actually he was closer to her than
anybody. He had been smitten with that raven-haired
woman preacher from Texas the first time he ever
saw her picture.

Bea Lamont, an exuberant and outgoing woman
preacher, who had befriended "The Addicts," had
shown it to him. "Look who's coming for a revival,"
she announced holding up a card.

John examined the card which contained a photo
and the notation, "Evangelist Anne E. Nethery, Corpus Christi, Texas." He smiled to himself. "I'm gonna
marry that girl," he remarked smugly.

Bea laughed. "Fat chance you've got, fella."

From the very start — even though their back-
grounds were worlds apart — John and Anne were attracted to one another. Some of their friends shook
their heads at the possible match-up — John, an ex-
con and heroin mainliner for sixteen years from the
Bronx and Anne, a gifted woman preacher who had
spent most of her life working in the church.

For some two and a half years, their relationship
ran hot, then cold, then hot again. Months drifted by
without any contact. Then, their paths would cross
again. Nothing would have changed. They were still
attracted to one another.

But once the prophecy came, the distance widened
between them. Like the other "Addicts," John

slipped. He made excuses for continual trips back to New York. "I gotta see Mama," he claimed.

Yet, Anne knew who "Mama" really was.

One night she drove from Pennsylvania into the Bronx looking for John who had called several days earlier. With the aid of Louis, a former addict, she located John's old territory of "Korea" and began driving up and down Westchester Avenue, across Simpson Street and down Fox Street.

At an intersection, a darkened figure staggered in front of Anne's car stopped for a redlight. Fear clutched at her when she recognized the stumbling man. It was John! She and Louis leaped from the car and piled the spaghetti-legged creature in the back. He was high, his eyes bleary and bloodshot, his words slurred.

"When we gonna get married, babe?" he mumbled.

Anne drove without answering. Her eyes riveted to the road.

"You know I love you, don'tcha."

She swallowed hard. "Yeah, sure you do."

"No, I mean it ... I really do ... no kiddin'."

Anne was irritated. She had had all of John Gimenez she could take. This was the end. All along she realized she was taking a sizable risk with John, an ex-drug addict who had flopped in the ministry. Her own ministry was on the line. Many people had told her to get away from John "before you're tainted too."

"Well, how 'bout it?" John pressed again. "When we gonna get married?"

Lights flashed as cars passed on the interstate. The highway had already crossed the state line separat-

ing New York and Pennsylvania. Highway 84 would
soon become U.S. 6. She would then turn towards
Coudersport about four more hours away. Anne
prayed silently that the night would end and John
Gimenez would be out of her life.

"Well, I'm waitin'," he said.

She sighed. "In about a month, John," she
answered quietly.

The answer seemed to settle the issue. In moments
John dropped off to sleep as did his friend. By six
o'clock the next morning, they pulled in front of
David Minor's white house. After a hurried breakfast, Anne left as quickly as she had come. She had
little reason to stay.

John remained behind. All through the few weeks
that followed, the lanky, sensitive pastor sought to restore his wayward visitor. "Come on, John," Brother
Minor enthused before each service, "You've got to
lead singing."

At first, he refused. But under the pastor's soft
touch, John was soon leading songs in church and
praying. As time passed, he had ample opportunity to
reflect on what went wrong. What had caused the entire ministry to come crashing down upon him.

"Lord, why do you have me here?" he asked, still
looking into the valley as the sun continued its de-
cline. "I hate this place. I'm from New York. There's
nobody I know up here. It's a drag. It's not my kind
of place."

Misery overpowered John and he crumpled to his
knees beside the bed. Tears — hot and stinging —
soaked his face and shirt. "Oh, God," he moaned.

As he cradled his head in hand, a vision unfolded

before him. He saw himself, dirty and completely caked in mud, lying on an Army cot. His hair was long and matted with dirt and lice. The cot appeared to be sinking in the mud.

Heavy metal bars reaching from floor to ceiling surrounded him. The cell had no door. John realized there was no way out of the place. He was trapped, locked away.

Next to him lay a decaying body — bloated, flesh rotting away, eyes sunken in. The stench of putrefying flesh assaulted his nostrils.

It was like a horror movie — fog swirling in and out of the cell, gnarled and barren trees hanging overhead. The mud floor seemed to belch and bubble like a bed of quicksand. The whole scene gave him a feeling of sinking.

"God, why?" he screamed, the words bouncing off the walls and echoing down what seemed an unending corridor. "Why have you forsaken me? Why have you forsaken me?"

The Word of the Lord — firm and sure — came. *"I have not forsaken you. Instead, you have forsaken Me."*

Then, at once John knew.

The dead body lying next to him was his old nature. He lived with that person. He talked with him. He took him wherever he went. The sixteen years of drug addiction. The prisons — Elmira, Sing Sing. The streets of the Bronx. He constantly testified about the past. Much of his present life lay rooted in the past.

"I've never given it up," John thought.

If the needle wasn't in his arm, it was still in his mind. He always talked about it. The play he had

written focused on it. They even used a real needle in
the play. The addict went through the whole scene of
shooting up ... taking out a glassine bag of white
powder ... pouring it into a bottle cap ... heating the
mixture ... drawing it into a needle ... wrapping
a piece of rubber tubing around his arm until
his vein swelled ... then injecting directly into the
swollen vein.

Every time that drama was presented, John lived
through the hell of being a heroin addict. His nose
ran, eyes watered, pulse quickened. At times, he even
felt "the rush" when the actor shot up.

Now the horror stood before his eyes. His backslid-
ing. His waywardness. The pride, the stubbornness.
God had wanted to deliver him from that grisly
weight. It was killing him. Unless he submitted, this
would be the end of John Gimenez.

"God, help me ..." he sobbed, reaching upward with
both hands surrendering to the Lord. "I give up ... I
give up ... please help me." Tears flowed as he groaned
in agony.

A shock almost like a powerful electric current
rocked his body. The Holy Ghost came down upon him
— as if a man had laid hands on his head. The power
of God surged through every fiber of his being.

"Ahhhhhhh!" he screamed under the power.

All at once, he was on his feet dancing, laughing,
screaming and speaking in tongues. "Glory!! Hallelujah!! Praise the Lord!!" A fountain of joy rose up
inside of him and burst forth in praises to God. He
sang and shouted until his throat ached. "He is Lord!!
He has risen from the dead and He is Lord!!
Glory to God!!"

Downstairs, Brother Minor heard John shouting and praising God. He knew that deliverance had come. He too joined in the worship session.

The chains and shackles had been broken from John Gimenez. The weight of iron had been lifted; the vessel cleansed. God's man was free at last. Now he was fit for the Master's use.

2

The Newlyweds

Three weeks passed. After preaching camp meetings in New Brunswick, Canada, and New York state, Anne arrived one night in Coudersport returning Pastor Minor's daughter, Sharon. While she was away, John had telephoned. Through the conversation, she sensed a welcomed calm in him. Yet at the same time, she was apprehensive and edgy.

Over the phone, John had said, "When you get back, we'll go ahead and get married."

Anne was frightened at the prospect of marrying an ex-drug addict who had lived a topsy-turvy life the last two and a half years. Even though they had talked frequently about marriage, she continually brushed aside any such talk as "serious" because of John's yo-yo lifestyle.

Light trickled from underneath his bedroom door as she approached it. She tapped softly on the door. "Yeah," he responded.

"It's me," she announced, opening the door.

John glanced up, his large, open face framed by a table lamp. "Hi," he smiled.

A curious look crossed Anne's face as she gazed into

his shining dark eyes. "Oh, he has changed," she
thought to herself. "There's softness and light in his
eyes." Peace flowed into Anne's heart. She knew that
John had had a genuine experience with God.

"I just wanta say, honey," he volunteered, "it's
really now or never."

Anne looked at him for a long moment knowing full
well he was asking her to spend the rest of her life
with him. What would she do? Instantly her thoughts
raced back to a church in South Bend, Indiana, where
they had met. Bea Lamont had invited her there to
see the play presented by "The Addicts."

When she arrived that night, the play had already
begun. Act two came. The curtains parted showing a
dark, heavy-set man, his dirty tee-shirt revealing a
huge potbelly, his hair disheveled and sprayed gray.
He swigged from a fake Vodka bottle.

Bea leaned over in the dark. "There's your future
husband," she suggested, a sly smile on her face.

Flabbergasted she would say such a thing, Anne
looked straight ahead not even bothering to reply.
"I'm 33 but I'm not desperate," she thought to herself.

Later, Bea invited the same man, John Gimenez,
along for a hamburger following church. Anne had
been worked on by the best matchmakers from
Canada to Texas. She never thought Bea was playing
that role.

As they drove, Bea spoke up. "Anne Nethery, what
are you doing with a man's hat in your car?" she
asked, pointing to a hat in the car's rear window.

"I bought it to spook people away from thinking a
single girl was traveling alone on the road," Anne
answered. "But since then, I've decided to use it like

Cinderella did the glass slipper. The first man that hat fits I'm going to marry."

Anne threw her head back laughing. But as she did, she caught a glimpse of John with the hat perfectly fitting him. He quickly pulled it off.

She never entertained the thought of seeing John Gimenez after that night in South Bend. Little did she know two and a half years later, she'd be considering marrying him. And that's the question she now faced.

Besides that, Anne knew marriage to John would mean total rejection from her family. She couldn't have both — John and her parents. The latter had repeatedly warned her against marrying him. It was an enormous decision.

Tears gathered in her eyes. Her heart felt as if it would explode. "It's now," she said tearfully. "It's now."

They sealed their pact with a kiss.

The issue of marriage was settled between them now, but there were other roadblocks. Pastor Minor had a few reservations. "I'm not against you folks marrying," he explained, "and I don't feel you can't marry. I'm just not sure if I'm the one to perform the ceremony. I need to feel right about it."

That was Monday night. Everybody agreed to pray about the matter. By Wednesday, Brother Minor announced he felt different. "I'm ready to get you folks married if you're still asking," he volunteered.

"Amen," John and Anne chorused happily.

Another thorny obstacle loomed in the person of Anne's parents. Thursday night, she telephoned her brother-in-law, Dick Campbell, announcing she was getting married the following night. "Tomorrow

night around eight, you tell my folks I'm married and
I'll call them in a day or so," she instructed.

Dick reluctantly agreed. Later he panicked fearing
his in-laws would blame him. He phoned them and
broke the news. Within minutes, Anne found herself
on the phone attempting to explain matters to her
parents. Already aware of John's problems — past
and present — the Netherys were dead set against
the marriage.

The conversation, calm at first, grew heated. "If
you go through with this ... if you walk down that
aisle and stand in front of that preacher, you'll see my
face," her mother warned, "and I'll be cursing your
marriage."

"Oh mother, I've lived single 34 years, almost 35,
and I can live another 35 or so if God wants me to,"
Anne answered.

"Well, why don't you marry a *white* man then?"
came the brutal reply.

Having been raised in a Texas city near the Mexican border, Anne understood her mother's feelings.
The product of Puerto Rican parents, John's physical
features were olive complexion, black hair and dark
eyes. He also spoke Spanish. The Netherys identified
all that as being Mexican and in their town Mexicans
stood last in the social structure.

John finally walked into the kitchen where Anne
clung to the receiver. Her body shook, tears flowed.
"Hang up," he urged, "hang up."

She shook her head. "No, they have a right to say
what they're saying," she said, covering the mouth-
piece with her hand. "They're trying to save my life."

Anne was a broken, despirited bride-to-be when

the phone conversation ended. She wept as John held her close and wiped the tears from her eyes. "Don't worry," he said softly. "You're not a child and I'm not a child. We know what we're doing. They have their lives to live and we do too."

Pastor Minor also added soothing words to Anne's troubled heart. "Sister, the Bible simply says honor father and mother," he reminded her. "I believe you've done that ... now we just have to leave the rest to God."

The wedding date arrived — September 1, 1967, the Friday before Labor Day weekend. Most of the bride and groom's friends couldn't attend since the wedding had been planned so hurriedly. Anne's friend from Elim, Sara Bright, came down to be maid-of-honor while David Hunter served as best man. Some fifty people from Brother Minor's church assembled in the meeting room of the old wooden house for the ceremony.

Through a mix-up, the wedding march was played three times before Anne finally made it down the aisle. John thought she'd gotten cold feet and wasn't coming. Before the service was over, Brother Minor, John and Anne were in tears from the impact of the moment. An overwhelming sense of God's Presence hovered overhead.

On the honeymoon, the newlyweds traveled to Hartford, Connecticut, and Anne ended up preaching a brief revival meeting. They were just visiting in the church when the pastor rushed up after service. "Oh, thank God, you're here," he enthused. "You're an answer to prayer."

"What?" Anne asked.

"You're the answer to prayer," he explained. "I've got a visiting preacher who's killing this revival and I need your help."

"Well, we *are* on a honeymoon," Anne responded. "We just came by for a visit."

"What about it?" the pastor pressed.

"If John thinks it's okay, I'll preach."

"Yeah, sure," he agreed. "Go ahead."

Anne preached the remainder of the revival. Then, they drove back to Coudersport, stopping off briefly at Mountaindale, New York, where John and many other addicts had first come following their conversions.

Back in Coudersport, the Gimenezes settled into a tiny, $50-a-month apartment near Brother Minor's church. As the days of the honeymoon came to an end, John awoke one day to discover he was married to a woman who freely spoke her strong convictions and opinions. Not to mention the fact she supported the family through her ministry. It was quite a bruise to his masculine ego.

Anne had to buy him a white shirt in which to get married in. They drove to *her* meetings in *her* car. In Detroit during a revival, they were introduced as "Evangelist Anne Nethery and *her companion.*" That introduction even bothered Anne.

Thus, their early days of marriage were characterized by countless instances of learning to flow together as one instead of two. In Peoria, Illinois, before a gathering of preachers, John was due to share his testimony. "Before I speak, I'd like for my wife to say something," he announced, typical of a newlywed showing off his wife.

Anne had been told the group was a meeting of evangelical pastors. She unwittingly construed it to be a gathering of Pentecostals. "Praise the Lord," she greeted the preachers, "God's moving by His Spirit in all the earth."

The preachers sat staring straight ahead. Anne thought to herself, "It's early in the morning. They must be half-asleep."

"It's just like Joel said He's pouring out His Spirit upon all the earth," she continued. "Great things are happening today."

The preachers glared back at her. A few yawned noticeably. "Boy, this is the deadest group of Pentecostal preachers I've ever seen," Anne thought. "I need to rear back and find something to move 'em."

"We just heard the other day that 46 Catholics at Notre Dame got filled with the Holy Ghost," she yelled with glee, "and they're speaking with other tongues as the Spirit of God gave utterance."

By now, John had realized her mistake. He dropped his head thinking, "she's either crazy or doesn't have any idea where she's at."

Anne finally stopped and took a seat. "Get me out of here as quick as you can," she muttered, figuring out she wasn't among friends.

In the meantime officials at Elim Bible Institute had contacted John about helping out with a giant outdoor crusade in Bogota, Colombia. His ability to speak Spanish would be a valuable asset to the team. Elim couldn't pay for the Gimenez' travel, however, they would have to raise the funds themselves. That posed another problem for the newlyweds.

Since Anne had been full-time in the ministry for

four years, God had always spoken first-hand to her about such ventures of faith. She didn't have a word from the Almighty about going to South America. Thus, she dug her heels into the ground over the trip.

"God hadn't said anything to me about going," she said flatly. "I don't believe we're going."

"I think we are," John replied.

She shrugged. "We'll see."

Over the ensuing several months, they collected missionary offerings to pay for the trip. All the while, Anne questioned and posed doubts. Up until the day before the trip, she was still dubious even after the passports and tickets came through.

Then, the day of departure arrived. She awoke early that morning to the voice of the Lord. *"You shall be going,"* He said.

It suddenly occurred to Anne that John had been right all along. Now that she was a married woman, it represented a lesson that God wouldn't always tell her first everything in the future. When John awakened, she confessed what the Lord had said.

As the trip turned out, though, she would have many opportunities to say, "I told you this wasn't God." But she knew better. There were problems from start to finish — airline delays, missing luggage, hotel mix-ups. It started when the Gimenezes flew from Miami to Barranquilla, Colombia. They were due for a two-hour layover for a flight to Bogota. The two hours stretched into six. Then the airline couldn't locate John's luggage.

"Well, you know all things work together for good," Anne suggested cheerily. "And you remember what David said, I will bless the Lord at all times."

"Humph," John mumbled.

In a flash, Anne quoted four or five more scriptures for the situation. John's dark eyes settled on her. "I know the scripture," he responded through clenched teeth, "get off my back."

Anne looked away briefly. As she did, the Lord spoke to her. *"Why don't you shut up; it wasn't your luggage."* Lesson No. Two in being a good wife, she thought, don't mouth scriptures when it's like a thorn in the flesh.

"I'm sorry," she said, turning back to John.

"It's okay," he nodded.

For a while John paced back and forth in the baggage area. Then he spotted a tall, seedy man carrying his bright plaid suitcase across the airport parking lot. "Give me my suitcase," he shouted, running after the man.

The startled man dropped the suitcase and fled. John quickly scooped it up. The claim ticket had been popped from the luggage but all of John's clothes — especially the two new suits Anne had bought — were inside.

Finally, they arrived in Bogota and got to the hotel. Nightfall had come. The Gimenezes were bone-tired from their travels. Anne surveyed the hotel room and especially the two twin beds. "Ask the attendant if he has a room with a double bed," she instructed.

John looked surprised. "I'm not asking him that," he said sheepishly. What'll he think?"

The attendant stood motionless, the Gimenez' bags still on his handcart. "I don't care what he thinks," Anne replied with a shake of her head. "It's 50 degrees outside. There's only a sheet and

bedspread on those beds ... and I'm not sleeping
by myself."

John turned to the attendant and explained in
Spanish that they were newly married. The man
looked at Anne, then back at John. A wide grin showing a bright gold tooth surfaced. Within a few minutes, the attendant had found a room with a large
double bed.

The next morning John telephoned Carlton Spencer of Elim. "We're here," he announced excitedly.

"You're here," Spencer responded. "What do you
mean you're here? Didn't you get the letter?"

Now it was John's turn to act surprised. "What
letter?" he asked.

"We wrote telling you not to come. There were problems with the meeting and we've had to cancel it.
We're just here trying to work out the details of re-
scheduling it."

John's heart sank. He hung up the phone and reluctantly explained the story to Anne. "You might have
been right all along," he suggested.

"Maybe so," she agreed, "but why don't we just wait
a few days?"

John nodded. "I guess so. There's no need in trying
to catch the first plane back to the states. We're here
and might as well spend a few days."

"I'm tired anyway," she continued. "I'd like to rest a
couple of days. Maybe God'll do something."

The temperature in Bogota averages about 58 degrees year-round. It's something like being in an "air
conditioned" city at an altitude of 8,600 feet. The
Gimenezes spent a day sightseeing among the gra-
cious Colombian people as well as dodging most of

Bogota's frantic "kamikaze" taxi drivers and pick-pockets. The two latter groups have gained world-wide attention for their proficiencies.

The next day they were invited to a missionary re-treat, La Mesa, back in the Andes Mountains. Want-ing to see the country, they quickly agreed. About seven o'clock that night, the Gimenezes and five others were riding in a large van along a rugged mountain road. The narrow roadway had been cut out of the mountain. Shear rock decorated one side. The other was a drop of thousands of feet. Palm trees below looked like toothpicks.

As dusk came, Anne grew anxious. "I'm glad this man knows where he's going in this rainy weather and darkness," she volunteered to John.

The driver, who had brought his girlfriend along, turned to the Gimenez' friend, Bob Barker, asking something in Spanish. "What'd he say?" Anne asked. "What'd he say?"

John smiled. "He just asked Bob if he knew where we were going because he's never been up this road before."

Anne's eyes grew wide. She looked anxiously from one side of the road to the other. "Look at that," she shouted, pulling at John's arm.

"What's the matter with you?"

"Look."

John peered ahead in the glare of the headlights. Then he saw Anne's reason for alarm — a gaping hole in the road apparently washed out by heavy rains. About the same time, the driver spotted the hole, too, and hit the brakes. The van fishtailed wildly off the road. Its rear tires — still spinning — dangled perilously over the cliff.

"God help us," the Gimenezes prayed.

Seven wobbly people gingerly crawled out of the van being ever so careful not to send the vehicle down the cliff. "We'll not get that van moved without a wench or something," Barker said surveying the situation. That came shortly though when a huge garbage truck rounded the curve and stopped.

"Don't you people know better than to be out here after dark," said one of the truck's crew as he walked up. "There were five people murdered around this same spot last week. Nobody comes out here unless they're running from the law."

Anne gulped at the man's words. "Thank you, Jesus, for your protection," she murmured.

The truck's crew connected a heavy chain to the van and slowly pulled it back onto the road. Everybody re-boarded the van but only after the driver had edged cautiously around the washout. Voices lifted in praise to the Lord as they drove to the retreat facility.

The Gimenezes stayed several days at La Mesa enjoying the scenic beauty of the mountains and the lush valleys below. One morning as John sat reading his Bible, the Lord spoke. *"Go back to the city."*

Then they gathered their belongings even throwing in some wet clothes Anne washed that morning. A rusty public bus filled with peasants and farmers of all descriptions and even a few chicken coops on top pulled up as they walked out to the road.

"Well, at least I feel comfortable in this bus — appearances or not," Anne remarked as the bus sped along the mountain road.

"Don't look now," John suggested, "but I just saw

the driver make the sign of the cross and start pumping the brakes like crazy."

"Ohhhh, not again," she moaned.

"Praise the Lord," John laughed.

As the Gimenezes walked into the hotel lobby, Johnny Isles, a young missionary from the states who Anne knew, stood checking out. Johnny was accompanied by Hector Pardo, who identified himself as a Colombian pastor. When he heard the Gimenezes were ministers, Hector insisted that they hold services in his church. Their return to Bogota proved to be the timing of the Lord. What followed turned out to be God's blessing.

Hector publicized the fact that Reverend Gimenez would be at his church. People throughout Bogota thought "Reverend Gimenez" was the well-known Puerto Rican evangelist by the same name. The church packed out. They would not be disappointed though.

John had taught Anne some scripture choruses in Spanish. She beat the tambourine and they sang. Anne preached while John interpreted. He also gave his stirring testimony. The people loved it. But best of all, God blessed.

Churches throughout the city opened their doors. Crowds followed from one church to another. Buildings jammed as lines extended to the sidewalks. The power of God manifested itself in many physical healings and miracles. One elderly man's deformed hand was miraculously restored as John prayed. Hundreds were converted.

Elim had leased a large apartment with five bedrooms for the planned crusade. Since it was unused,

the Gimenezes were invited to stay there. A former
missionary to Cuba, Sixto Lopez, who now had a radio
ministry in Bogota, also stayed at the apartment with
his wife. He casually mentioned one afternoon that
Pat Robertson, president of the Christian Broadcasting Network, would be in town shortly to negotiate
the purchase of a radio station.

John smiled at the news. He had met Pat, as well as
Demos Shakarian, back in 1965 during a Full Gospel
Businessmen's airlift to London. John's team of "Addicts" had led many drug users from the Soho district
to Christ. He and Pat had also appeared on television
together.

Sure enough, Pat arrived in a few days looking, as
John remembered, for all the world like the late President John F. Kennedy. After finalizing his business
in Bogota, Pat made preparations to return home.
"Whenever you're back in the states, get in touch
with me," he suggested. "There's a genuine revival
going on in Tidewater Virginia ... and I'd like to have
you folks as guests on the '700 Club'."

"Sure," John agreed.

Neither John nor Anne had any idea how God was
orchestrating their lives and future. Only in looking
back could they see the importance of Pat Robertson's
simple invitation.

3

An Answer To Prayer

The Gimenez' brief stay in Bogota turned into six weeks of extended ministry before they returned to the states in January, 1968. They both had speaking dates scheduled in Texas — together in San Antonio, John in Houston and Anne in Corpus Christi.

She desperately wanted John to visit in Corpus Christi but the problems with her parents still lingered. Since their marriage, Mrs. Nethery had addressed all letters to Anne using her maiden name. "I'll never acknowledge you're married," her mother wrote.

Anne suffered under the strain. At times, it was like a stabbing pain in her heart that wouldn't go away. Many nights she lay awake — unable to sleep because of the stress. "If I could get just one prayer answered, Lord," she prayed continually, "I'd like to have this situation resolved with my family."

Before leaving for Texas, John reached a decision. "I'm not going to force myself on your family," he decided. "I won't go down there and make them meet me. I'll go on to Houston, then I can fly down to Corpus. We'll pick up our new car, do the speaking date in

Orange and go back to Pennsylvania."

Anne agreed. They did a week of meetings in San Antonio, then Anne drove to Corpus Christi while John flew to Houston. While in town, she telephoned her parents and later visited briefly showing them photographs of their trip to South America.

Before leaving to stay with a friend, her dad warmed up. "Since you're in town, why don't you come over and spend Wednesday night," he suggested.

Anne hugged his neck. "Okay, if that's what you want," she said.

"Sure we do," he smiled, emphasizing the "we." Mrs. Nethery was quiet.

Anne preached that Wednesday night, then drove to her parents' house. When she reached the front door, her dad was waiting. "Hurry, hurry," he said excitedly. "John's on the radio."

She was puzzled. "He must mean John's calling on the telephone," she thought, following her dad into a back bedroom. Her mother lay across a bed listening to the sound of John's voice over her powerful FM radio.

"I didn't know John was going to be on the radio," Anne volunteered.

"Sh-sh-sh-sh-sh," her parents insisted.

For another hour or so, Anne and her parents sat listening intently to John's testimony. Anne marveled at what God might be doing. Somehow her mother had turned across the radio dial beaming John's voice from 200 miles away. She heard the name "Gimenez" and turned back to listen. Then, the Holy Spirit went to work.

John's appearance on the radio talk show had been arranged by the pastor of the church where he was ministering. His time had been limited to a few minutes. In it, he shared how God had delivered him from the hells of drug addiction ... how the Lord was blessing his life ... how God had worked miracles in South America.

As John shared, the telephone rang in the studio. People had questions for the converted drug addict. In the meantime, nine o'clock came and with it the radio station's power was boosted. It reached a full 200-mile circle from Houston. That circle now included Corpus Christi ... and his in-laws.

"Here's a fairly hot question," the announcer briefed John. "You've been talking about how God handles problems. Don't you have any problems or trials that aren't solved?"

John took a deep breath. "Yeah, sure I have problems," he began. "In fact, I'm in the middle of one right now. My wife is in Corpus Christi while I'm here. We're not together because she's visiting her parents and they don't want me there. I'm Puerto Rican and an ex-drug addict and they feel their daughter has made a big mistake in marrying somebody like me.

"That hurts for somebody to be prejudice against me. Yet when I look at it closer, I realize I might feel the same way if my daughter married a guy who'd been a dope fiend from New York. I'd probably be upset too. So I do have problems ... and a few testings too.

"But I believe that the day will come when my in-laws realize I love them and we'll be a family to-

gether. They'll see I genuinely love their daughter
and mean her no harm — only good. I've never met
them but I understand how they can feel the way they
do, but I'll love and respect them no matter what."

A warm glow rose inside Anne as she heard John's
heart-rending words. She realized miracles were
underway. Something had happened.

The next day Anne's mother telephoned. "It's your
father's idea," she emphasized. "When John comes
down here — by the way — when is he coming?"

"He'll fly down on Saturday. We're trading in my
old car and then leaving on Monday."

"Well, your father wants you to bring John to the
house," her mother mumbled.

"Okay," Anne answered.

Anne, her only sister, Jean, and brother-in-law,
Dick, picked up a feverish John Gimenez at the Corpus Christi Airport. For weeks, John had been
plagued by the flu bug. They drove to the Campbells'
house before going out for dinner. "I'm worn out,"
John announced, his head spinning from the flight
and the flu. "I think I'll rest a while before supper."

Since they'd picked him up from the airport Jean
had reacted distantly to John. In fact, she had con-
demned Anne's marriage for months as well. But she
grew concerned over John's sickly condition.

"What's the matter, John?" she asked softly. "Is
there anything we can do?"

"I don't know ... maybe pray," he suggested weakly.
"I've just had this flu and can't seem to shake it."

Suddenly, the Presence of the Lord filled the room.
Jean sprang out of her chair speaking in tongues.
John felt like he'd been struck by lightning as she laid

her hands on him. Healing came instantly.

Her own opposition to John ceased with the healing. But God had more miracles up His sleeve.

When the two couples arrived at the Netherys, Anne's father was standing with the screen door open, a wide smile on his face. "John, I heard you on the radio the other night," he announced warmly, clasping his son-in-law's hand in a firm grip.

Anne's mother acted graciously too. The radio program had been used as a sovereign act of God. The Netherys' walls of fear and prejudice were broken down by the Lord's compassionate touch. And the Almighty had honored a word spoken to Anne just a week before.

While in San Antonio, Anne continued to struggle over the problem with her parents. The trip to Corpus Christi loomed ahead. The difficulty hung like a leaden weight upon her.

One night following a service, an old friend brought her an encouraging word. "You're God's child and He loves you," the friend assured her. "He's going to do something you want very much. And it's going to be very quick too."

And so it was.

4

"I Know Where There's An Empty Church Building..."

Orange, Texas, was due to be the Gimenez' last stop before returning to Coudersport. A three-day meeting had been scheduled. John had preached both nights although Anne had shared briefly in her usual fiery manner. About an hour before the final night's service, someone rapped on the door. Anne was showering so John went to the door.

Outside stood the pastor's wife and another woman from the church. "I need to have a chat with you, Brother Gimenez," the pastor's wife announced timidly.

"Sure, come in," John greeted them.

The two women walked in and took seats near the window. "Ah, I don't really know how to put all this," the pastor's wife began anxiously.

"Well, just go ahead and say it the best you can," John assured her.

She took a gulp of air. "My husband sent me over here to tell you that the church doesn't want your wife speaking from the pulpit anymore," she blurted out.

"I see," John replied.

"You can introduce your wife, but she's not to give

any kind of word from the pulpit," the woman
continued.

"Is that all?" John asked curtly.

"Yes," she answered.

"Okay," he said, opening the door for them to leave.

By the time Anne finished showering, John's temperature had risen considerably. "Did you hear the
message I received?" he asked heatedly.

"I got part of it," she nodded.

"Evidently these people don't believe in a woman
having a ministry," John said, his temper growing.

"Obviously not."

John picked up the phone and started dialing.
"What are you doing?" Anne questioned.

"I'm calling the preacher and canceling the
meeting."

Anne shook her head. "Wait a minute, honey. Put
the phone down."

He stopped dialing, thought for a moment, then
placed the receiver back in its cradle. "Okay, now
what?"

"This man didn't put me in the ministry and he's
not going to take me out. If we leave, he'll just say
we're inconsistent and untrustworthy."

John walked to the motel room window and looked
out. "What do you suggest doing then?" he asked,
turning back to Anne.

"Well, they've made it plain I'm not welcome, so I
won't go to church tonight. You go ahead though and
do whatever God leads you."

He was quiet for a few moments. "You're probably
right," he said finally, "but I still don't like it."

That night John responded to the pastor's request

to give his personal testimony. At the Holy Spirit's inspiration, John took his listeners into the depths of drug addiction...the pain, the sorrow, the heartbreak. People throughout the congregation wept openly as he shared his personal hell of 16 years standing.

Then he told the poignant story of walking into Damascus Church on 162nd Street after being released from jail and finding Jesus. People were immediately on their feet shouting and praising God. Many sat in amazement at the miracle God had done in John Gimenez' life.

As they sat back down, John brought the message to a close. "What would you think if I told you everything I've just said couldn't be true?" John asked.

People were stunned. A few looked around unsure of what he'd said.

"In some peoples' books, that's the way it would be because I got saved under a woman's ministry and some people can't accept that," he continued. "They believe a woman isn't supposed to be a minister. And if that's what you believe, you'll have to forget conversion stories like mine or else chalk them up as God's mistake."

With that, John walked off the platform and out of the church. No one moved. People sat in stunned silence. He had left his audience, particularly the pastor, with a lot to ponder.

As they drove back to Coudersport, Anne wondered if she would be facing more serious challenges to her ministry. Only time would tell, she thought. She knew and believed one fact above all — God had called her to the ministry.

The first Wednesday night back in Coudersport the
Gimenezes were seated in church when Brother
Minor walked back to them and began praying. The
prayer suddenly ran into prophecy.

"I am sending you forth to a people you know not of,"
the prophetic word declared. "There I shall make you a
great blessing ... and I shall bless you mightily."

Anne had previously spent about three months
pastoring a small church in Corpus Christi. Her suc-
cessor was leaving the church and had invited them
to come as pastors. The prophecy settled that question though.

"We can't be headed to Corpus," John remarked
afterwards. "The prophecy said we were going to
a people we don't know. And you know those people
in Texas."

"Right," Anne acknowledged. "God must have
something else in mind."

Throughout the spring and into early summer, they
traveled in meetings with Anne doing the lion's share
of preaching. John mostly gave his testimony or
shared experiences from his life with scripture references. While in Coudersport, he borrowed a copy of
the movie, "Way Out," and used it in getting many to
make decisions for the Lord.

Months before, John had written Pat Robertson
about his availability. A July date was settled upon
for him to appear on the "700 Club." John gave his
testimony and as an added treat he and Anne sang
scripture choruses. Their reception from the public
proved warm and enthusiastic. Their most popular
song, "The Devil's Mad and I'm Glad," was an im-

mediate favorite.

Anne's use of a tambourine inspired local sales of the instrument. Most Tidewater music stores including the stamp redemption places exhausted sales of the items after the Gimenezes appeared on the "700 Club."

One morning while still in the Tidewater area, John awoke from a strange dream. "You won't believe what I dreamed last night," he told Anne over breakfast.

"Well, tell me," she said, her ears perking up.

He took a swallow of orange juice. "I dreamed I went to the mailbox and got out a big white envelope. When I opened it, there were two tickets to Bogota in there."

"Ohhh," she said, her voice falling. She arched her eyebrows in that familiar pattern. "I'm not all that interested in making a returned trip to South America."

That night as they viewed the "700 Club," Pat Robertson made an unusual announcement. "I'm planning a return trip to Bogota, Colombia. We'll be ministering in several places besides completing arrangements for the purchase of a Christian radio station."

"Wow," John exclaimed, clapping his hands. "Isn't that something."

He walked to the telephone and dialed the "700 Club" number. "Tell Pat that I had a dream about getting two tickets for Bogota in the mail," he announced. "I don't know how it's going to happen but I believe God wants us to go with this group in October."

When Pat got the message, he relayed it over the air with a wry smile. Days later — to everybody's surprise but John's — someone handed over the airfare for the Gimenezes to make the trip.

They spent the month of August in meetings around Detroit where they celebrated their first wedding anniversary. They returned to Tidewater early in September for a busy month of speaking engagements, an autograph party for John's book and another appearance on the "700 Club." CBN had also arranged several places for the Gimenezes to minister — one of the places turned out to be a popular Charismatic church in Newport News.

John had planned for Anne to minister the first night of the three-day series. However, the church's leadership had evidently already heard about Anne's preaching. That night, a young man from the church arrived to drive them to the service.

"Brother Gimenez, the pastor wanted me to remind you of our doctrinal position regarding women in the church," the young man mentioned as he drove along.

"What's your position?" John asked.

"We hold to the words of I Corinthians 14:34-35 which says that a woman should keep silence in the church," he said mechanically.

"Ah," John responded, drawing a deep breath. "I see." He looked back at Anne sitting in the back seat. She shrugged her shoulders.

That night as they walked into the church, the pastoral team and elders sat on the front row. "Good evening, Brother Gimenez," they greeted moving over to give John room to sit. Anne stood momentarily waiting to see if they'd make room for her. When they didn't, she walked back to another aisle. "I must be an invisible person," she thought to herself.

All three nights Anne received the identical treatment. Nobody acted as if she were even present. The last night as they backed out of the church's parking lot, the pastor walked over. "Thanks for being with us, Sister Anne," he enthused.

"Oh, you're welcome," Anne smiled sweetly.

As they drove away, Anne shook her head. "I've had rank sinners treat me with more kindness than these people," she said.

"I know, honey," John replied, reaching over to take her hand. "They were just threatened by you ... and when people are threatened, they act differently."

At times, Anne wondered if this was only the beginning to her problems as a woman preacher. First, Orange, Texas. Now, Newport News. What next?

One afternoon while John attended a meeting, Anne sat chatting with Dorothy Baxter whose house they were staying in. "I really wish you folks would stay in this area and start a church," Dorothy remarked.

Anne smiled, never saying a word.

Inwardly, she asked herself, "A church? That's so strange for her to suggest that. She doesn't know us. I've never preached here and John has only testified. Why would she say such a thing?"

That night before bed, she told John what the woman said. "God showed me we will know where to stop and where to plant ourselves because He'll give us an empty church building," John responded.

Anne laughed. "You think there's an empty church building just setting around waiting for you?" she questioned.

"Honey, I know God spoke to my heart," he said softly.

Several nights later they drove from Denbigh where they were staying into Portsmouth across the James River Bridge. As they walked in through CBN's glass doors, a smiling, bespectacled woman approached Anne. "I know where there's an empty church building," she volunteered. "Would you and your husband be interested?"

Seldom at a lost for words, Anne stuttered, "T-T-Tell him."

"I know where there's an empty church building," the still-smiling woman repeated to John. "Would y'all be interested in seeing it?"

"You bet," he said heartily. "When can we go?"

"I'll find out and call you," the woman, who identified herself as Betty Forbes, promised.

Arrangements were hastily made to see the building Saturday afternoon. First, the Gimenezes had an autograph party at Long's Bookstore in Norfolk. As it turned out, Betty Forbes couldn't drive them to the building so she sent her best friend and fellow Methodist, Hazel Sasser.

"I haven't been able to get in touch with anybody about the building," Hazel explained, "so I don't have a key. But we can still look the place over if that's okay with you."

"Fine," John answered. "Let's take a look."

Anne didn't respond. She simply went along for the

ride — fully expecting to find a dilapidated building complete with broken down roof and shabby exterior.

She was wrong though. A well-kept, white frame structure greeted them from the corner of Lens Avenue and Kitchener Avenue in Norfolk. Even without a sign posted, the Gimenezes knew it was a Pentecostal church. They had seen hundreds of similar buildings during their travels.

Mayme Farr, Betty Forbes' mother, lived directly behind the church on the street paralleling Lens. She knew Hazel would be bringing the Gimenezes to look at the building. "Hello, everybody," she called out, walking around the structure, "can another soul join the party?"

"Sure, come on," John laughed.

John and Anne strolled around the tidy church holding hands like a couple of sweethearts. "Isn't it beautiful," Anne suggested as they peered in the windows.

"Yeah," John sighed, drinking in the comfortable-looking sanctuary.

Hazel and Mrs. Farr were still chatting on the front lawn when the Gimenezes finished their walk around the building. "Why don't we pray," John suggested, "and just commit this to the Lord."

The four linked hands. Hazel and Mrs. Farr bowed their heads. John and Anne raised their voices in unison. "Oh, God, whatever you want. If this is where You want us, Lord, we're willing ... just make us know God ... we praise You and thank You for the answer."

Hazel looked uneasy when the loud praying stopped. So did Mrs. Farr. John sensed they weren't accustomed to that fervent petitioning of the Almighty. "If we come here, that will change," he thought to himself.

"We're leaving for Bogota in the morning," John explained to Hazel, "But we'll be back next Saturday night. Is there any chance of getting a key to this place?"

Hazel nodded. "I'm sure there is. I'll call Betty and see what she knows about it."

The Gimenez' second trip to Bogota came the following week. Upon returning they were anxious to hear about the building situation. A telephone call to Hazel established that a key would be available Sunday afternoon to get into the building.

And sure enough, that was the case. Brother Mason, an Assembly of God minister, showed them the building. Hazel, Betty and several of their friends came along to pray.

Brother Mason explained the situation. "In years past the church had been packed by a husband/wife team of Pentecostal Holiness preachers," he said. "Later, they built a larger church and sold the structure to the Assemblies of God who attempted to start a mission in the building. Since the area was already heavily churched, the mission failed and the denomination put the building up for sale."

The Gimenezes stood in the aisle listening to Brother Mason, a short, friendly man, while surveying the facilities. Songbooks and offering pans stood neatly in place in the pews. Tables and chairs decorated the Sunday School rooms. A baptistry and public address system completed the sanctuary. A pastor's office was housed in the rear. The only things missing were a pastor and a congregation.

Several of the people had already walked through the building laying hands on the pews. Then, somebody suggested, "Why don't we pray." Everybody agreed.

A message in tongues came forth as everyone sought God. Brother Mason interpreted. *"The Lord has this day set before you an opened door,"* he declared, *"and you should step through in lively faith believing in His Name ... trust Him ... believe Him ... obey Him."*

The Gimenezes were impressed with the facilities. They felt the touch of God through the prophecy. Both realized they needed to move forward. Yet a snag materialized almost immediately to use of the building.

Brother Mason made it clear the Assemblies of God wanted to sell the building. "We plainly have no need for it," he said flatly.

"Is there a possibility your group would rent us this building until we see if a congregation would develop?" John asked.

Brother Mason rubbed his chin and thought for a moment. "Tell you what," he volunteered. "Call me back tonight and I'll try to find out if the board will consider renting the place."

That night following church, John telephoned Brother Mason but ran into a brick wall. The answer was no. The church board was prevented by state law from considering such a matter for at least three weeks.

John walked back to the car discouraged. "Let's go get our clothes packed," he announced glumly. "We're going to Atlanta tomorrow."

"What did the man say?" Anne asked, feeling a twinge of disappointment.

"He handed me something about a business meeting in three weeks," he shot back.

They drove to their night's lodging and got ready for bed. Anne wouldn't let the matter rest though and telephoned Brother Mason. "I didn't quite understand what my husband said about the situation," she began innocently. "Could you explain it to me?"

Taking great pains to explain the problem, Brother Mason said, "Sister Gimenez, the full board of the church has to vote on this matter. It'll take three weeks before we can do that. That's the law of the state and I can't change it."

"Oh," she responded.

"Quite frankly," he continued, "other people have asked to rent that building and the board has always voted no. There's really not much reason for them to change their minds now."

Anne thought for a moment. "Well, would you consider renting the building for the next three weeks for us to have an evangelistic meeting? We'll clean it up. It would be safe from vandals because it's setting empty right now. We would take full responsibility."

"Well ..." he began.

"Just consider renting us the building while you're waiting on your meeting to decide if you can rent it?" Anne asked sweetly.

"I tell you what," Brother Mason suggested. "I'll have to call everybody on our board and I won't be able to complete that until tomorrow night. Why don't you or your husband call tomorrow night after nine o'clock? I'll try to have an answer by then. Okay?"

The whole thing sounded illogical. Why rent a building for three weeks before having a meeting to decide if you would rent it? But on the other hand, it just could be God's way of doing things. At least that's the way Anne explained it to John.

Instead of leaving for Atlanta the next day, the Gimenezes stayed over. That night shortly after nine, John called Brother Mason. "I don't understand it," he said, sounding puzzled. "But the board has agreed to rent the building until they can have a business meeting to decide whether or not to rent it. You can come over and pick up the key."

"Wonderful," John shouted.

That night the Gimenezes were staying with Jim and Tammy Bakker, who worked with CBN at the time. Everybody was excited about what God might be doing. The next morning, Tammy and Anne were in the kitchen having breakfast. "I wonder what do I do next?" Anne asked out loud.

"The first thing you do is call Vepco — the power company — and get the electricity turned on," Tammy commented, beginning to pick up breakfast dishes.

"Right," Anne agreed. "Without power, there's no meeting."

"In more ways than one," Tammy giggled.

Anne quickly looked up Vepco's number and dialed. "Lady, that's considered commercial property and it takes about ten days to get the power turned on," came the mechanical answer. "It has to go through city inspection."

"Isn't there anything that can be done?" Anne
questioned. "We want to have a revival meeting in
the church beginning this Sunday night."

"I have no control in the situation," came the reply.
"The only thing you can do is call City Hall. Talk to
the City Inspector. It's all up to him."

Anne hung up. "It's not up to any old City Inspector," she muttered. "It's up to my Father." She and
Tammy prayed briefly about the problem. Then she
dialed the City Inspector's number and explained the
situation. Surprisingly enough, he promised, "I'll be
there tomorrow, lady."

It seemed as if Anne hadn't heard him. "We've just
got to have this power turned on because of the
revival service," she rattled on.

"Lady, I'll be there tomorrow," the inspector
interrupted.

Still, Anne hadn't heard. "We just need it desperately for our meeting," she continued.

"L-A-D-Y, I'll be there tomorrow," he said emphatically. "Your lights will be on by four o'clock."

By now, Anne had gotten the message. "Praise
God," she rejoiced. "Tammy, I think the Lord's in this."

"I think you're right," Tammy agreed.

Sure enough, the electricity was flowing on
Wednesday night when the Gimenezes drove to the
little church. But that wasn't all that was flowing.
Something was in the air. A kind of stirring.

About thirty people showed up to clean the place
that night. They felt the stirring too. Everybody sang
praises while floors were swept, windows cleaned and
pews dusted. God's house might be a little empty for
the upcoming Sunday afternoon service but it would
be clean.

5

3101 Lens Avenue

A tiny ad appeared in *The Virginian-Pilot* newspaper. It said: "Revival meeting with John and Anne Gimenez, 3101 Lens Avenue, beginning October 20th."

As they drove to the Sunday afternoon meeting, Anne spoke up. "You gotta remember that nobody knows us in this area," she reminded John, "and there might just be a handful of people."

"True," he answered with an agreeing nod.

"So don't be discouraged if that's the case," she continued.

He gave her a knowing glance. "No, don't worry. I'll witness to one just as well as a thousand."

"I just don't want you to be disappointed," she repeated, reaching over to take his hand.

"Fine," he replied.

John turned off Lafayette Boulevard onto Lens Avenue and drove past a white-frame church building. Cars lined the street. The building looked packed. People streamed into the structure. "That can't be our place," he said, driving further down the street.

Another two or three blocks passed. "I think you'd

better turn around," Anne suggested. "We've obviously missed the church."

He wheeled the car around New Yorker-style and drove back to the first building they'd seen. "That *is* our place," he announced, excitement mounting. They walked into the church almost fearful. Neither had any idea people would turn out in such numbers.

Camp meeting-style revival followed the next two weeks. People got saved. Many were healed. Countless others were filled with the Holy Spirit. Spirit-filled believers — like Hazel Sasser and Betty Forbes — from the nearby Fairmount Park Methodist Church brought their friends from near and far. God moved sovereignly.

By the end of the second week, the Gimenezes were convinced God's hand lay upon their venture of faith. Still, they had heard nothing from Brother Mason about continued use of the building.

One afternoon Anne telephoned her mother with news of God's blessings. "And we've found this beautiful little church that'll seat 250," Anne gushed, "and it's tailor-made for what we need. The only problem is the people who own it want to sell."

"Don't buy it," her mother suggested, as the phone lines jangled with static.

"Why not?" Anne questioned, startled at her mother's boldness.

"God just makes me know in my heart that building isn't big enough for what He's going to do with y'all in that area," her mother replied confidently.

"Hmmmmm," Anne mused.

The conversation eventually lapsed into small talk about family and friends. But afterwards, Anne couldn't get away from her mother's words. "Where could mother come up with thoughts like that?" she pondered. "Could it be God?"

Brother Mason called one evening asking the Gimenezes to meet him the next morning for coffee. "We've heard that God is moving over there in the little building," he said with a smile. "The blessing of the Lord is evidently on what you folks are doing."

"Amen," John agreed. "I don't think we've had a night without people being saved and filled with the Holy Spirit."

"Praise God," he enthused. "That's beautiful."

"It's really been great," Anne remarked. "People have been coming from all over to the services."

Brother Mason paused for a moment, took a sip of coffee and cleared his throat. "Well, we've had our meeting," he announced with a grin, "and the board has decided to rent you the building."

"Oh, hallelujah!" the Gimenezes chorused, hugging one another, then reaching to shake Brother Mason's hand.

"This is beautiful," John commented, "just beautiful."

"But," Brother Mason continued, gesturing with his hands, "the building is for sale and we'll make every effort to sell it — including a for-sale sign on the lawn."

Anne and John exchanged smiles. "That's no problem," John responded. "God's led us this far. He's put us here and we'll just have to trust Him to take care of the building situation."

Provision of the rented building stood like a guidepost to the Gimenezes. They knew it was time to begin regular services at the still unnamed church. At the next meeting, John announced a Friday night gathering for those people interested in making "this place your church home."

Friday night came. John expected 40 or 50 people, but only 15 showed up occupying the first two rows of the sanctuary. And it was a skeptical, negative group at that.

"We don't know if you're going to be here another six months or leave," one man suggested. "It looks kinda unstable to me."

"I don't feel I should give up my church for this," another woman prompted, gesturing her hand toward the empty pews.

"I've been in my church for years," said one woman, "I just can't give it up."

John's expectations were sinking as one by one bowed out. Most of the people said they'd attend but couldn't make it their church home. Even Betty Forbes, who'd suggested the meeting location in the first place, said she couldn't make a change now. It didn't look like much of a beginning.

John glanced at Anne who had been silent most of the meeting. She gave a faint smile. Then he stood. "Well, folks, God has been speaking to me and He's said this is the place He's called the Gimenezes to. Whether all of you come or none of you come — as for me and my house — this is where God wants us and I know it."

The Word of the Lord grew inside of John as he shared from his heart. "God said we're going to build on the solid rock. The rock that is Jesus Christ. He's the rock we're building on."

Now he felt a sense of certainity in God. The anointing flowed. The words were surely prophetic when they came out. *"We're going to call this Rock Church ... and the gates of hell will not prevail against it. This will be the foundation stone upon which many lives will be built. I know it will."*

He paused for a moment allowing the words to sink in. Then, Hazel Sasser raised her hand. "I'll stay and help," she volunteered.

John looked into her cherubic face. "God has done something in this woman's life," he thought, remembering how he had needed a pianist once at CBN and she was afraid to play "without music." He had prayed over her. She had never been the same since that prayer.

The meeting closed shortly afterwards.

John and Anne Gimenez were now the pastors of Rock Church in a rented, white frame building at 3101 Lens Avenue, Norfolk, Virginia. They had one official member, Hazel Sasser, their pianist.

6

Trials, Tests and Temptations

Since returning from Bogota, the Gimenezes had lived in several locations around Tidewater staying with various friends who had spare bedrooms. But after making the decision to launch Rock Church, they needed to get an apartment in the Fairmount Park section of Norfolk near Lens Avenue. That would save needless driving.

"I have an extra unit not being used," a slender, dark-headed woman volunteered after services one Sunday. "You can live there for nothing."

"Praise the Lord, we've been praying about a place," John rejoiced.

The Gimenezes gratefully moved into the tiny upstairs apartment near the church. That lasted for a couple of months. Then one day, Al and Joyce Manby approached John. "There's a small attic apartment in our home," Joyce announced, "and we'd love for you and Sister Anne to come and live there."

"I thank you for offering," John responded. "but we're already staying in another place the Lord has provided."

"Oh," she said, sounding disappointed. "I was so

sure the Lord had told us to mention this to you."

In fact, the Lord had done precisely that. Within a few days, the generous woman who had "loaned" the apartment suddenly asked the Gimenezes to leave. "I'm renting that apartment," she said distantly, "and I'd like for you folks to be out by the end of the week. I need to get the people in who've rented the place."

John and Anne felt badly. They knew they were being put out. Yet they also saw the hand of the Lord making provision for them. Collecting their meager belongings, they relocated to the attic apartment at the Manbys. They were pleasantly surprised. As it turned out, the new attic quarters were roomier than the one they vacated.

"It was a real temptation to say something to that woman," John remarked to Anne the first night in the new apartment."

"Yeah, I know what you mean," she agreed. "But I think her husband forced her into it. He always seemed money hungry anyway."

"True," John acknowledged, reaching over to turn out the light. "I'm just glad for God's hand to be in the situation — three steps ahead of everything and everybody."

Spiritually hungry people began finding the little church on Lens Avenue. There was a magnetism about the place. Many came looking for more of God. They were quickly fed.

Finances were always tight though. The Gimenezes got whatever was left over after the bills were paid. At times, that meant anywhere from $10 to $50 a week — never any more. They survived mostly from the sales of John's book and outside speaking

engagements. That frequently bought groceries.
Sometimes people even left bags of groceries at
the door.

Both pondered thoughts of returning to the road as
traveling evangelists. That was the only life Anne
had known for the last five years. John enjoyed the
adventure of traveling. At least the finances were
better going from church to church than simply
pastoring a single church.

Some of their friends thought they'd made a mistake in settling down. "Do you really think it's God
that would settle you down to pastor 50 people or so,"
friends constantly asked, "when you could reach
thousands otherwise?"

The Gimenezes had only one real answer. "We
think it's God's will." No other answer really mat-
tered. From a financial standpoint, their actions
didn't make sense. They had just begun getting
bigger and better meetings. Their incomes grew
proportionally.

Yet something special was taking place at the little
church on Lens Avenue. A flow was developing between John and Anne. When he led the singing, she
preached and vice versa. A blending of two distinctly
different styles — John's compassionate soul winning
and Anne's dynamic preaching — produced a refresh-
ing, positive and joyous approach to the Christian life
that many earnestly hungered after.

"You know, if it's God's will for us to stay here," John
suggested one day, "I think you'd get pregnant. With
us more or less settled down, this would be the right
time for you to have a baby."

Anne smiled knowingly. Just a few days earlier, she

had laid that fleece before the Lord. "Well, I am 35 and not getting any younger ... not to mention the fact that you're 36."

"Yeah, we won't mention those facts especially since we're both having birthdays next month," John laughed.

Within a couple of weeks, Anne became pregnant. They both began to feel more confident about being in Tidewater. Two months slipped by seemingly with no problems for Anne. A few people wondered if the Gimenezes hadn't waited too late for her to be having a baby.

Then one Friday she was due for her first doctor's appointment but had to cancel because of a car problem. Sunday morning she preached — so typical of Anne — challenging and enthusiastic. That afternoon, she felt movement inside her stomach.

"It's as though something is breaking loose within me," she explained to John. In a few hours' time, she was passing blood.

"We better call the doctor," John decided, a worried expression creasing his face.

Anne described her symptoms to her doctor. "There's nothing I can do for you," the physician said tersely. "I suggest you get in bed and stay there. You may stop bleeding or you may lose the baby ... but if you do there's no way I can prevent it."

Obeying the doctor's instructions, John helped her into bed, but nothing seemed to help. Early Monday morning, John rushed her to the hospital. He stood beside her bed clutching her hand tightly and praying with all his might.

The hemorrhaging grew worse and, in the end,

Anne lost the baby.

Several weeks went by. Still recovering from the miscarriage, Anne sat one evening in the attic apartment with John watching a flickering black and white movie from the 1940s. It was the story of an emotionally ill woman who had been committed to a mental hospital. Years before, she had lost a baby. While she was in the hospital, she searched in vain for the infant.

As the story unfolded, Anne noticed, John grew quiet. Then tears came. All of a sudden, he placed his head in his hands and sobbed. The freshness of their loss struck close to John's heart.

"John ... honey, it's okay," Anne said softly, putting her arm around his quivering shoulder.

He wiped away hot tears. "Why? Why?" he cried. "Why did we have to lose the baby?"

Anne pulled him close. "Honey, we can't ask why. All we can say is Lord, I delight to do Your will. God, you know best and we praise You for all things."

"I know ... I know," he sobbed. "I just wanted a baby ... something that was an expression of our love...." His words trailed off.

Tears formed in Anne's eyes. She was equally grieved over losing the baby. For months to come, she would ask herself, "Why? Could *I* have done something to cause the miscarriage?" But today she would be strong for John's benefit.

"God will work it out," she said, reassuring him. "I know we'll have a baby someday. I know we will."

Losing the baby came as a heavy blow to the Gimenezes. Another one — just as tough — followed close behind. They always seem to come in pairs.

CBN had been an important booster. The Gimenezes had appeared a number of times on the "700 Club." Without question, most people in Tidewater knew about them from the Christian network.

A CBN official called one day setting up an appointment. "Since you folks have begun a church in Tidewater, CBN will have to cut some of its ties with you," he informed them.

"Why's that?" John asked, surprised at the man's words.

"Well, when you first came to us, you were in a traveling ministry," he explained. "Now you're pastoring a local church in the community. From our standpoint, we can't treat you any differently from any other church in the area."

Then, the official leveled the *coup de grace*. "And besides that, women preachers aren't thought of too highly in this area."

Although John didn't expect any favored treatment from CBN, he was hurt at the mention of "cutting ties." The put-down about women preachers also bothered him. It seemed like someone was forever offering a belittling remark like that.

"I don't understand it," he said afterwards.

Anne smiled. "Honey, I think this is God," she assured him.

"What? God? How can you say that?"

"If we succeed, we'll do it because it's God," she shared. "If pastoring this church isn't what God wants us to do, we'd better find out now."

"Maybe you're right," John conceded.

Little did the Gimenezes realize that more trials, tests and temptations lay ahead. They would come to learn that struggles always preceded God's blessing.

7

"Are You Ashamed of Me?"

The drug culture was making heavy inroads into "middle class" America during the late 1960s. Popularized by the new psychedelic music and glamorized by avant-garde celebrities, the culture relocated from ghetto areas of northern metropolitan cities. Towns from Bangore to Bakersfield and Seattle to Surfside were now faced with the problem. Tidewater Virginia — seven hours by car from New York City — was no exception.

Almost from the first day he came to the area, John Gimenez saw the signs of heavy drug trafficking. Skilled at talking the language of the street, John handed out gospel tracts, rapped with kids and led many of them to Christ. He didn't wait for problem kids to come calling. He readily sought them out.

Word spread throughout Tidewater's drug culture about John's testimony. Many drug users, hippies and other assorted outcasts came to Rock Church just to "check him out." Their visits always produced unusual results. Miracles often occurred.

Once a bare-footed, long-haired boy, high from drugs, wandered to the front of the church during a

baptismal service. Glassy-eyed, the youth stumbled
and fell into John's arms.

"Satan, I command you in Jesus' Name to release
this boy," John shouted, looking sternly into the
boy's eyes.

"AH-AH-AH-GA-GA-GA," he moaned.

Many in the church began praying loudly. Some
spoke in tongues. "Praise the Lord ... Glory to God ...
Thank you, Jesus."

The boy started gurgling and flailing about with
his arms. John tightened his grip. "In the Name of
Jesus, I command you to release this boy, you evil
spirit," he demanded.

As the church and John continued praying, the
boy's twisted expression changed. A smile crossed his
lips. His darting eyes grew calm. Two deacons helped
him to a front row seat. Before the service ended, the
boy confessed Jesus as his Saviour.

On another occasion, a teenage girl, who had taken
a drug overdose, was brought to the church. She was
barely breathing, her pulse faint. The Gimenezes
stopped the service when the girl was brought in.
"Our job is to pray for people," John told the crowd.
"Let's look to God and believe Him for a miracle ...
right now."

John and Anne both laid hands on the girl praying
fervently in the Spirit. Then, the miracle came. The
girl was healed instantly by the power of God. People
stood in the aisles waving their hands and praising
God for His mighty acts.

The girl, an attractive blond with a sweet personality, experienced a wholesale change in her life, gave
up drugs and became an honor student. Then, her

mother intervened. "You will not go to that holy roller church ... no matter what," her mother vowed.

In time, cut off from the church, the girl slipped back into her old lifestyle. John couldn't understand it. "How could a mother want her daughter on drugs more than attending Rock Church?" he often asked himself.

Through such encounters, John committed himself as never before to helping troubled kids. It represented a burning desire in his heart.

Conoly Phillips, a successful Norfolk car dealer, would play an important role in John's efforts to aid problem teenagers. A nominal church-going Presbyterian, Conoly had met the Gimenezes on their last trip to Bogota. A thin, soft-spoken man, Conoly had taken the trip more out of curiosity than anything else. Yet during the week in Colombia, he encountered the Lord in a fresh, new dimension. He came back to Norfolk a changed man.

John had shared with Conoly about the possibility of staying in Tidewater and starting a church. Through their conversation, John bared his heart — telling about his 16 years of drug addiction as well as his burning desire to help young people on drugs.

It turned out to be a fast friendship. Conoly was impressed with the Gimenezes and enthused about John's vision. "I'll be glad to help anyway I can," he volunteered.

Thus after returning from Bogota, John kept in frequent contact with his new friend. As the drug culture spread into the high schools, Conoly volunteered to get John before the public to sound the alarm about the problem. His solid reputation in the community served as a useful tool in getting John before civic groups and high school assemblies.

The school systems as well as many social and fraternal clubs opened their doors to the converted addict. Soon people were calling from near and far just to get John to lecture on the drug problem. Naturally, he always included the source of the "cure" — Jesus Christ.

Conoly's willingness to help deeply touched John. In turn, he wanted to do anything possible for his friend whose overriding concern was his unsaved wife. She loathed his new-found religious zeal. Most of all, she detested his association with John Gimenez.

For months, Conoly attempted to get her into a service at Rock Church. "Just go and see what it's like," he coaxed.

Finally, she agreed.

Drummond Thom, a preacher from South Africa, had been invited to speak the night Conoly and his wife came. John had never met Thom before but naturally assumed he'd be a respectable, dignified Britisher. He should have known better.

That night, John planned to sing all the "right" songs and do everything in a proper, harmonious atmosphere. He didn't want to do anything to upset Conoly's society-bred wife. He took a quick offering. "Don't want her to think we're after people's money," he thought. Anne didn't even play the tambourine.

Then it was time to introduce the speaker.

"We are deeply honored this evening to have Reverend Drummond Thom with us," he began, trying to find the biggest words his fifth grade education could

employ. "He is a learned man, a man of profound bi-
blical knowledge and wisdom."

John noticed several people in the audience yawn-
ing as he buttered up the speaker. "Now may I present
the Reverend Drummond Thom," he said.

To John's utter dismay, Thom, a tall, hulk of a man,
leaped across the platform screaming at the top of his
lungs. "Praise the Lord!! Glory to God!! This is the day
the Lord hath made!! Let us rejoice!!"

John was horrified — totally unprepared for the
visiting preacher's booming voice. It vibrated from
wall to wall like a ricocheting bombshell. The building seem to shudder under Thom's thundering explosion. John thought his eardrums would literally
burst.

"I don't need a microphone," he bellowed. "I've got a
built in microphone. Hallelujah!!"

Back and forth, Thom paced across the platform —
exhorting, shouting, praising the Lord. John put his
hands across his eyes. He couldn't look. He knew all
his efforts to placate Conoly's wife had failed.

Thom finally ended his sermon by throwing his
Bible on the floor and jumping on top of it. "I stand on
the Word of God," he yelled. John summoned enough
courage to look back at Conoly's wife. Her face was
ashen. Conoly's head was bowed. He knew his efforts
had bombed. She wouldn't come back to Rock Church.

John wondered to himself, "Have I lost Conoly
as a friend?" He was still bemoaning the situation
when the Lord spoke. *"Are you ashamed of Me?"*
He whispered.

"Ashamed?" John thought. "Am I ashamed of
the Lord?"

In an instant, his old life flashed before him. He had come from the dung heaps of society, the cesspools, the garbage pits. All he had ever known was filth, dirt and drugs. Once he had even worn foul-smelling rags on his feet they were so badly swollen. His needle-marked arm had festering, runny sores. He slept on the roofs of decaying tenement buildings and in dark, damp basements. Dirty cardboard boxes often covered his body.

That's where he had come from. God had delivered him from the gutter. He could not be ashamed of what God had done. He could only rejoice. He knew the power of the Gospel in his life. It was freedom and liberty — not coldness and sterility.

He leaped from his chair and ran to the altar. Hungry, searching people crowded the front. He and Thom moved in the power of the Holy Spirit ministering salvation, deliverance and healing. God was no respecter of persons and John couldn't be either. It was a great lesson for John to learn.

Some four months after Anne suffered the miscarriage, the telephone rang one afternoon. David Minor's wife, Lorraine, was trying to reach John. She and Anne exchanged pleasantries for a few moments. "It's funny talking to you," Lorraine said, "I just had a dream about you last night."

"You did?" Anne questioned, her interest rising.

"Yes," Lorraine answered. "I was doing some ironing in the dream when you walked up to my bedroom door. You were holding a dark-haired baby. I said 'Well, Anne Gimenez, whose baby is that?' You answered, 'She's mine and she's four months old'."

Anne laughed. "Well, I'm still trying," she assured Lorraine.

Ever since she had lost the first baby, Anne had prayed for another child. She had claimed Psalm 37:4 because the baby was "the desire of her heart." Unknown to her at the time, she was pregnant and Lorraine Minor's dream of a dark-haired baby would prove uncannily accurate. In fact, Anne would call it prophetic.

Throughout the summer of 1969 and into the early fall, John operated at an exhaustive pace. His speaking engagements took him before various civic groups and schools. People frequently asked what church he pastored. In turn, that brought people — adults and kids — to the doors of Rock Church. Sometimes the kids came first, then the parents showed up to discover what had made such a difference in their offspring. The little white-framed church on Lens Avenue began to fill with happy, joyous people.

By October, John's ministry among Tidewater drug addicts had become so extensive a former private school house on Old Kempsville Road was leased. Known as Proclaim, the center received gifts of money, furniture and food as soon as it opened. Juvenile courts in Norfolk and Portsmouth began referring teenagers to Proclaim. Several area narcotics squads dropped off addicts rather than sending them to jail.

One juvenile court judge declared, "John Gimenez' work is the most effective effort in Tidewater for

stemming the rising tide of drug usage." Such state-
ments created more work for John.

Not only did Proclaim monopolize John's time and
attention, so did his activities with "The Upstairs," a
Christian coffeehouse in Virginia Beach. Open seven
days a week, the place drew a curious blend of clean-
cut Christian youngsters as well as seedy-looking
hippies. On Tuesday and Thursday nights, John
headed for the coffeehouse after services at Rock
Church. Many times he wouldn't get home until two
or three in the morning.

Slowly, Anne became resentful of John's all-
consuming activities outside the church. She felt God
wanted their efforts centered around the church —
not dispersed in three or four different directions.

She complained one day about John's lack of interest in the church. "That's where God's placed us," she
asserted, "and that's where I believe we're supposed
to center what we're doing."

John shook his head. "Look, you take the church
and pastor it," he responded. "I'll run the youth program. I just don't want any part of the church. It's too
confining … the people are too demanding. Besides,
that's your ministry anyway."

"Nothing doing," she said emphatically, placing her
hands on her hips. "I'm not going to pastor the church
without you. I'll end up with a church full of old
women."

"Well, I'm not going to pastor it," he retorted. "I'm
leaving that in your hands."

Anne believed John's focus on the youth work was
wrong. It surely didn't coincide with a word God had
spoken to her two weeks before she met John. At the

time, she had wondered if she would ever marry. But one day God spoke during prayer.

"Daughter, I'm going to give you someone to walk by your side, hold your hand and share the joys and sorrows of the ministry with you," the Lord said.

To Anne's understanding, that meant she and John should be sharing the ministry together, not her with the church and him with the youth ministry. She persisted. At times, the conversations became so heated John walked out slamming the door behind him. Anne frequently wound up in tears. For a 36-year-old pregnant woman, who had had one miscarriage, it produced continual stress.

John felt he couldn't relate to some of the older and middle-age people coming to the church. He much preferred the street-wise kids of Tidewater. Being a kid at heart, he identified with their simple, happy-go-lucky ways. Even though he didn't realize it, John's problem stretched back to his old days as an addict. In that world, the addict ignored the demands and responsibilities of life. Older people constantly made demands upon John as pastor of Rock Church. Inwardly, he wanted to slip away from their claims on him.

Once before, God had taught John a crucial lesson over respecting persons. Now as he attempted to shift the pastoral role solely to Anne, the Almighty would intervene again unexpectedly. A showdown would surely ensue.

8

Divine Intervention

Anne felt that John always had time for everyone but her. Being pregnant and alone often, she continued struggling under the problem. One afternoon she drove to the Proclaim Center to talk with him. Several people were seated outside waiting for appointments. Knowing the couple he was counseling, she opened his office door.

"Excuse me, please," she interrupted. "I'd like to know when my husband will have some time to talk with me?"

"I don't know," John answered, looking up from his desk a little embarrassed at her entrance.

Anne fumed, tapping her foot anxiously.

"If you'll wait, I'll see you in a few minutes," John offered lamely.

"No, I'm leaving," she said angrily, walking out and slamming the door behind her.

For Anne, it seemed as soon as she overcame one problem with John's ever-demanding activities, another sticky situation cropped up. The telephone rang incessantly. People always wanted counseling, or the police had an addict in tow. Once she changed to

77

an unlisted number but that didn't last long. The
police as well as the welfare department uncovered
the number and distributed it freely.

As John slowly sank under the load, his temper
flared one night. "Why don't we just chuck the whole
thing and go back on the road?" he roared. "This pressure's getting too much ... I can't stand this."

Anne looked up. "Just one question, John?" she
replied.

"Yeah."

"Is that your idea or God's?" she probed.

He glanced away. "No comment."

Anne preached through her eighth month of preg-
nancy, but she remained healthy — free of any complications. Robin Anne Gimenez, a dark-haired,
dark-eyed girl — just as Lorraine Minor had seen in
her dream — was born on January 30, 1970. The
Gimenezes had the child they had prayed for.

John's shoulders would bear a heavier load in the
church now with Anne caring for the newborn baby.
As a result, the Proclaim board of directors hired a
staff assistant, Jake Johnson, who came from another
drug program in New York City.

"Well, at least, you'll be spending more time at
home with your family now that you've got some
help," Anne suggested, after hearing about the new
employee.

"Hope so," John agreed.

Even though he spent less time at the Proclaim
Center, John began noticing a problem whenever he
was around. He frequently brought kids into the center for help but they seemingly wouldn't stay long. At
times, he saw a few of them back on the street. He

recognized several kids were doing drugs again.

John realized his new assistant, Jake, was a domineering type. He didn't connect the problem to Jake until one day when he arrived at the center. A newly converted addict, who'd had a long history of drug problems, practically knocked him down coming out the door.

"Hey, what's up?" John asked.

The addict pushed past him. "Get lost, creep," he snarled.

"What's the deal?" John shouted after him.

Battered suitcase in hand, the youthful addict, his long hair blowing in the wind, crossed the street and began thumbing. John watched as a pickup truck stopped and the youth climbed in back.

"I better check this out," John decided walking back in the center. Jake chatted on the phone as he entered, his feet propped on the desk.

"I'll call you right back," the curly-haired assistant said hurriedly, hanging up.

"I think we've got a problem here," John began, taking a seat.

"What's that?" Jake asked, sounding indifferent.

"We seem to have no problem with kids coming into the center, but they don't stay long. They're leaving in a hurry without getting the help they really need."

Jake shrugged his shoulders. "Well, they're breaking the rules around here and I can't have that," he suggested mechanically. "Without rules, there's nothing but chaos."

"Oh, brother, you don't mean that," John offered.

"Yeah, I do."

"But you can't kick these kids out for breaking

some rule," John said softly. "You've got to have compassion. They're coming from the gutters. You can't expect them to be super-saints overnight."

"No?" Jake questioned. "Well, I think that's a mistake. I believe I'm doing it the right way."

John smiled faintly. "But you're doing it without compassion though," he said.

Toying with a pencil, Jake drew a deep breath. "Look, John, I'm not here to learn from you. I'm here to teach you ... you're really a novice at all this. You've been an addict but you've never run a center for addicts."

John stood up and walked to the door. Turning back, he said, "I don't mind learning, Jake, but I know God put me here with these kids. That's my ministry and it's based on compassion. If you can't work with compassion, you're not going to work at all."

Jake slapped the pencil on the desk and stood. "I think you're wrong," he said stiffly. "You can't let addicts dictate the terms. You've got to have rules."

Four months passed. Proclaim's board agreed Jake should find employment elsewhere. Once again that left the total job back in John's lap. More conflicts surfaced.

The board had been broadened to include a number of businessmen, who although wanting to help, didn't understand John's approach. Most of them felt John should raise the funds, bring in the addicts but leave the administration to the board. John struggled along for several months trying to keep the ministry together.

In the spring Anne flew to Corpus Christi to spend some time with her parents and show off Robin, who was now four months old. She attempted to call John several times without finding him at home or church. Finally, she reached Hazel Sasser.

"John's not here," Hazel volunteered. "There's been a problem."

"What's the problem?" Anne asked, sensing trouble.

"He resigned from the Proclaim Center and left for New York. He said he was going to visit his mama."

Fear gripped Anne's heart. She mechanically thanked Hazel and hung up. "New York ... mama ... drugs" rolled around inside Anne.

The bottom had dropped out. She was in Texas. John had a problem and headed to the only place he'd ever known — New York. Fearing what her parents might think, Anne didn't tell them. But she prayed as fervently as she had ever done in her life. The Gimenez' marriage, the future of Rock Church, maybe even John's salvation, hung in the balance.

9

"Arise and Build"

Late that night, Anne telephoned John's mother in the Bronx. Since Robin had been diagnosed with bronchial asthma, she left word for John to return her call. "There's an emergency," she instructed, "and I need to hear from him as soon as possible."

The next morning John called. "Hi, honey," he said sheepishly. "It's me."

Anne didn't ask a single question. "John, the baby is real sick," she began softly, "and I really need you down here."

"What's the matter with Robin?" he asked.

"She's developed a bad asthma condition," she answered. "The doctor says I can't leave with her until she's vastly improved. Why don't you just catch a plane and come down here. I'd feel a lot better with you here."

"Sure, hon, I'll get the next plane," he volunteered.

The following day John flew into Corpus Christi for a tearful but happy reunion with his family. Later he poured out his frustrations and hurts over the direction Proclaim had taken. "I resigned, went out to the car and started driving," he explained. "Before I knew it, I was already in New York."

"Well, sweetheart, I think God's allowed you to come to this place," Anne suggested.

John nodded. "I guess you're right. It's almost like I knew that once I got to New York. I saw the old neighborhood, the crime, the dirt. I knew I couldn't turn back to that — especially just because of the Proclaim thing. God has done so much for us and the church ... not to mention our baby." Tears came to his eyes.

Anne leaned over, brushed away the tears and kissed him softly. They held each other for a few moments.

"I really feel God has intervened for a special reason," she continued. "He wants you to accept the spiritual leadership and oversight of the church. You've talked about what you've been saved from. I think God wants you to major on what you've been saved *for*."

John was quiet. "I know you're right," he said finally. "My love for this youth work — even my emphasis on my past — had to come to an end."

"But I don't think it'll be the end of the youth work," Anne offered. "I just think we'll be based in the church ... that kind of ministry just ought to come from the church. As for your testimony, I think the Lord's just shifting the emphasis ... that's all."

"It's exciting," John enthused with a smile, "isn't it?" The Lord must really have something in mind for Rock Church to make such dramatic changes. Huh?"

"Yeah, I believe He's got great plans," she predicted.

Almost immediately, a fresh, new wind of the Holy Spirit began moving at Rock Church. A year or so before, the Gimenezes would be praising the Lord and there wouldn't be another voice worshiping or hand raised in the whole place. Now people were breaking free from the old rigid molds. They worshiped and praised God with abandon.

One evening the Gimenezes drove up to the church for services. Cars already ringed the building 30 minutes ahead of time. They chatted for a few moments. "Well, praise God," Anne shouted suddenly.

"What's up?" John asked.

"The Lord just spoke to me saying the windows of heaven are open over this place," she rejoiced. "We're going to experience an outpouring of the Holy Spirit."

"Hallelujah!"

And that's the way it all began. New faces showed up each Sunday. Friends like Betty Forbes made Rock Church "their home." God continually poured out His blessings upon the little church on Lens Avenue and to whoever came searching.

Freddy Jenks and his wife Carol both had bad drug habits they were desperately trying to kick. Carol, who was eight months pregnant, had been told the baby she was carrying was dead. Doctors had been unable to detect a heartbeat for weeks.

They came to church, were saved and filled with the Holy Spirit. John baptized them in water soon afterwards. The very next day Carol was rushed to the hospital where she delivered a perfectly healthy ten-pound boy.

Each time these miracles occurred, people learned to walk in a sense of expectancy of what God could do. And at Rock Church the Almighty seemed to be working overtime.

One Sunday morning, the Lord gave Anne a vision as she sat on the platform. She saw a hand pull a window shade down and then release it. The shade rolled all the way to the top as bright sunlight came streaming through the window.

Then, the Lord gave her a prophetic word concerning what she'd seen: *"The stigma over the Baptism of the Holy Spirit will be lifted and rolled back. Light will come flooding in."*

Within a month, a series of articles on the Jesus Movement captured the pages of *Life* magazine and the interest of the nation. Rock Church became flooded with people — more than 75% of them under age 25. The Jesus Movement had hit Tidewater.

The little structure on Lens Avenue had been built to hold 250 people comfortably, but now 350 were jammed into every nook and cranny. People sat everywhere — in the choir loft, adjacent Sunday School rooms, in the aisles. At times, extra chairs were even placed on the platform. The Gimenezes frequently had to step over and around people as they preached.

Crowds grew so large the building was becoming a fire hazard. Without question, Rock Church would soon have to find larger facilities.

All kinds of suggestions were advanced for what the church should do. It seemed like everybody had an idea. Then, local realtors had ideas too — vacant churches in Norfolk and Portsmouth, an abandoned theatre or two. The Gimenezes and the church's deacons looked at a number of buildings without finding anything suitable. Finally, John and Anne decided to get away for a few days to hear from the Lord.

They drove to Toronto for a convention, but for some reason ended up arriving the last day of the event. On their way home, they decided to stop off and visit friends at Elim Bible Institute in Lima, N.Y. Many of them had not yet seen Robin.

The Gimenezes hoped to see their friend, Costa Dier, the gregarious missions secretary at Elim. Since Costa is such a world traveler, they automatically figured he'd be globe-trotting. Sitting in the dining hall, they were talking with some people when Costa's son, Salem, walked through.

"When your father comes back, tell him we said hello," John shouted.

"Why don't you do it yourself?" Salem laughed. "He's down in his office."

Costa was his laughing, jovial self when the Gimenezes popped into his office. He had kisses and hugs for everybody. They shared with him about God's mighty blessings in the Tidewater area.

"That's beautiful," Costa agreed.

"But, we need some answers, brother," John said seriously. "That's basically the reason we took this trip to hear from God. We've been seeking God as to what our next step should be. We're thinking about buying and renovating an old building ... but we're just not sure."

Costa's eyes lit up. Standing, he exclaimed, "Brother, let's pray."

The Gimenezes linked hands with Costa's heavy grip. Everyone prayed fervently in the Spirit for several minutes. Then, the Word of the Lord came to Costa.

"Arise and build," he proclaimed, *"for I have called*

thee to build a tabernacle unto Me. Build for the thou-
sands ... arise and build ... arise and build."

"Praise God!!" the Gimenezes shouted. "Thank you,
Jesus!!"

Costa hugged them both. "I wish I could be with you
because there's going to be a spiritual explosion in the
Tidewater area," he said. "That's why you're to build
for the thousands. Get ready ... you haven't seen anything yet."

Costa's prophetic word had come on Friday. Sunday
morning, John and Anne explained to the church
what they had received from the Lord. "God has met
us," John told the overflowing congregation, "and
said we're to build ... build for the thousands."

The people stood together and applauded the Word
of the Lord. That morning, John received the first
building fund offering for Rock Church.

Even though the church had no property and not
even architectural plans for a building, the venture of
faith was begun — simply at the Word of the Lord. It
would become a principle for the Gimenezes and Rock
Church.

The next day when he awoke, John noticed a car
parked at the curb on Woolsey Street. It looked suspi-
cious so he decided to investigate. Walking outside,
he found Frank Perkins, an infrequent visitor at
church. "What's up?" John asked, crawling into the
front seat.

"I felt like I needed to come talk to you," Frank
volunteered.

"Sure, go ahead."

"I want to say this to you," he began sheepishly. "I
love you and I believe you're a sincere man. You really

believe in what you're doing."

"Thanks."

"But," he concluded, accenting the word, "what you're doing is not God."

What do you mean it's not God?" John asked.

"God isn't stupid," he suggested. "He knows that things are tight. God knows that money isn't fluid today."

John smiled and looked out the car window. The little three-bedroom house God had provided recently caught his eye. Somehow he never thought he'd own a nice brick home but God miraculously had made it possible. Faith stirred inside him.

"Brother, to tell you the truth, I've never heard of fluid money," he admitted. "I don't even know what it means. But whether money is fluid or not, we've heard from God. The enemy tries to lead you astray but we — Anne and I both — have heard the voice of the Lord."

Frank shook his head. "Well, I think you're making a big mistake. It's not God to build."

"Looks like we'll both find out, won't we?" John replied, getting out of the car and walking back to the house.

Not long afterwards, Bob Barkley and Jim Spiers — two men they had met years before in Colombia — visited in the Tidewater area. Over dinner one night, the two men, both well-known in full gospel circles, heard about Rock Church's plans to build.

"Well, anybody that's hearing from God knows that He's not telling anybody to build anything today," Spiers retorted. "The time for building churches is over. That's not God."

The Gimenezes were surprised. Spiers was highly respected by many people, even regarded as a prophet by others. They weren't shocked when someone like Frank Perkins questioned their plans, but Spiers was a different story. Could they be wrong?

No one spoke around the table for a few moments. Then, John cleared his throat. "Brother Jim, I don't know how God is speaking to everybody else today," he said confidently, "but God has spoken to us to build."

"It's really not a question of we think we've heard from God," Anne continued. "We know we did. There's no doubt in our minds."

Spiers chuckled. "Well, you go ahead and build but I guarantee that's not what God is saying today."

In time, John and Anne came to see encounters with people like Frank Perkins and Jim Spiers were necessary testings for every decision they made in God. The decisions had to be tried in fire. They were frequently driven to their knees praying for correct motives. But once they were agreed as one, the decisions never proved wrong.

This was the photograph of
evangelist Anne Nethery that
Rhea Lamont showed John.

"The Addicts" with John at the wheel of the van.

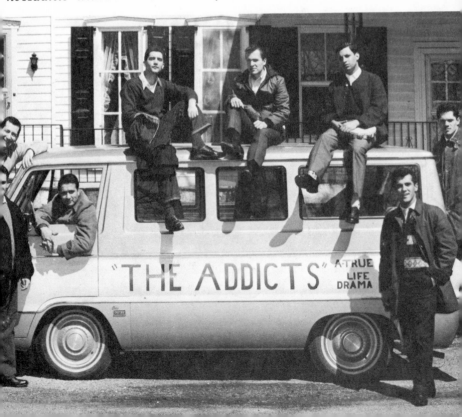

*Nicky Cruz, center, with Joh
and another member of "The
Addicts" in London.*

*"The Addicts" singing. Shorty Yeaworth, who produced the
movie, "Way Out," is pictured on the back row with his hand on
John's shoulder.*

The Gimenezes on their wedding day – Sept. 1, 1967.

menezes' first publicity

John and Anne lead a ch[...]
over the "700 Club."

The Gimenezes on the "700 Club" about 1968. Jim Bakker, now of
PTL, second from left, hosted the program that night.

101 Lens Avenue.

The Gimenezes at Proclaim Center.

The Gimenezes with their baby girl, Robin.

Rock Church
3101 LENS AVE.
SERVICES:
TUES. AND THURS. 7:30
SAT. YOUTH NIGHT 7:30
SUN. SCHOOL 10:00
SUN SERVICES: 11 A - 7:30

REV. JOHN ... ANNE GIMENEZ

*Robin outside
the church.*

Inside and outside photographs of the first sanctuary on Kempsville Road.

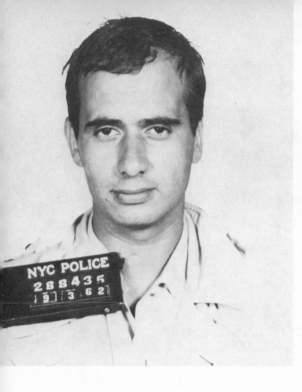

*This is John's last mug sho[t]
which was given him by an
agent.*

The Gimenezes the day the first sanctuary was dedicated.

ple jammed the newly constructed sanctuary.

balcony was added later, yet
ore worshippers came.

Congressman Whitehurst cut the ribbon. The Gimenezes were all smiles.

The Spirit flowed the day the new education building was opened.

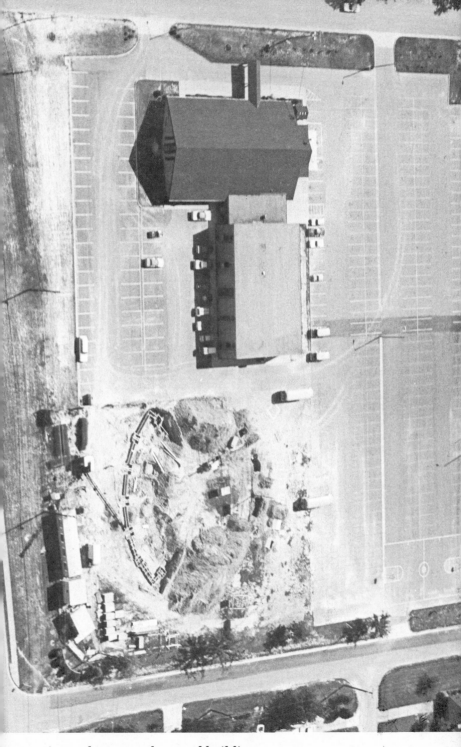

...nstruction underway on the round building.

Crane lifts cross on top of the newly-completed building.

Steel girders reflect the round shape of the new sanctuary.

Dedication day in the round building.

nne Gimenez leads in worship.

Pat Robertson interviewing the Gimenezes.

John doing a song with the Rock Church choir.

An aerial view of Rock Church on a Sunday morning.

Pat Robertson, president of C.B.N., Demos Shekarian, International President FGBMFI, and John Gimenez during National Steering Committee meeting – Washington for Jesus

A favorite at Rock Church – the Gimene.

10

Following The Spirit's Bidding

Bill Baldwin and his wife, Doris, attended Rock Church and knew about the search for more space. A real estate agent, Bill called one afternoon asking John to stop by his office. "I have something to show you," he promised.

In his paneled office, Bill had a sprawling map of Tidewater covering the side of one wall. Placing an index finger on the map, he said, "This is the very center of Tidewater right here ... and this is where the building corridor is going. Thousands of homes will be built here."

"Hmmm," John acknowledged. "That's interesting."

"Here on Kempsville Road," Bill continued, running his finger along the building corridor line, "There's a piece of property — five and a half acres in all. It's prime land. The owner's asking about $60,000 or $70,000 but I think we can get the price down."

John smiled. "This gets better the more you go along."

"Would you be interested in seeing it?" Bill asked.

"Sure, let's take a look," John responded.

Picking up Anne, they drove to the site. Over the years, the five and a half acres had become a dumping ground for people's unwanted junk. Rusted pieces of metal, broken glass, empty paint cans dotted the property. The Gimenezes even noticed a few snakes wiggling through the overgrown weeds.

The land fronted Kempsville Road, which at the time was a single-lane road with steep ditches on either side. Kempsville High School and a small Presbyterian Church stood in the distance.

"Well, I'm leaving it mostly up to you," Anne remarked to John.

Bill laughed. "That puts the whole decision in your lap, John," he said.

As he stood weighing the matter, John remembered that a struggling Pentecostal Church was located a few blocks away. The pastor had recently suffered a heart attack. Some of the members had left for Rock Church while a bickering faction remained to fight the pastor. John winced at the thought of locating on Kempsville Road and possibly hurting an already-weakened pastor.

"I guess we'll just think about it some more," he finally told Bill.

After a week or so, the Gimenezes began looking at other sites, yet to no avail. The five and a half acres stayed in John's thoughts, even though he couldn't imagine ever needing that much land. He even went so far as to take Fred Brenner, another preacher — who was looking for property — to see the site.

"Listen, John, if you don't grab this property, I might get it for my congregation," Brenner told him. "You're missing something if you let this go."

"You really think so?" John questioned.

"I sure do."

A spark slowly ignited inside of John. "Could this be the will of God?" he pondered. It clearly seemed the Spirit's leading. No other doors had opened. Even though there were no booming words from heaven, John felt peace with the idea of purchasing the land.

Anne also agreed with the decision. That was vital. They next presented the matter before the full church. Responding to the occasion, the people gave $5,000 in love gifts for the property's purchase. A $40,000 price was negotiated for the site.

No sooner had the property issue been seemingly settled when another offer presented itself. John received a telephone call from Joe Templeton, a businessman whose wife attended the church. "I'd like to give you something," Templeton announced.

"Great," John replied.

Driving to a Virginia Beach shopping center with Templeton, John was startled at the man's offer. "I want to give you three acres along here," he said, pointing to a grassy strip of land. "I'm going to develop a large shopping complex and I want you to have this for your church."

John looked at the grassy strip, then back at Templeton — hardly believing his words. "I'll have to pray about this," he responded cautiously.

"You want to pray about this?" Templeton asked.

"Yeah," John said. "I'll have to talk it over with my wife and a few of the deacons too."

"Well, okay," Templeton replied, "but don't look a gift horse in the mouth."

"Right," John answered, feeling pressured.

When he arrived home, Anne had supper nearly cooked. "What was Templeton's big news?" she asked, looking up from setting the table.

"He's just offered us three acres of land … free," John smiled. "The only thing — he wants a guarantee we'll build the church there."

Anne stirred a pot on the stove. "John, it sounds good, but God didn't tell us to build over there. God told us to build on Kempsville Road."

"But he's giving us a piece of property worth $3,000 for nothing," he interrupted.

She slapped a lid back on the pot and looked at John. "I don't care if it's worth a million dollars. God didn't tell us to build there."

John knew she was right. Templeton's deal looked good on the surface, but God's will had already been established. Why go against that. The Almighty never proved to be wrong.

Picking up the phone, he dialed Templeton's office. "I'm sorry," he began. "I appreciate your offer but we can't accept it."

"What?" Templeton shouted. "Are you people crazy?"

"No, we're just trying to obey God," John said simply.

"But I'm giving you something *free*! You don't have to pay for it. Can't you understand that?"

"Yes, sir," John answered, "and we really appreciate it. But we just can't accept it."

"You people are nuts," Templeton screamed, slamming down the receiver.

As soon as contracts were signed for the property, the church applied for a use permit from the Virginia Beach Planning Commission. Problems materialized quickly though. Nearby residents somehow believed John would use the site for a drug rehabilitation center. That belief spawned many unfounded rumors.

Petitions circulated to keep Rock Church out of the Kempsville Road site. Neighborhood meetings were called to mobilize support. The protest grew louder.

In August, the Planning Commission held a hearing on the use permit, deciding to defer the application for 30 days and instructing the planning staff to further study the request.

On Septmeber 1, 1970, the Gimenezes attended a neighborhood meeting in the hopes of presenting a balanced view of Rock Church. Rumors abounded that the church was composed of nothing but drug addicts, prostitutes and other misfits of society.

About a hundred people gathered in a nearby elementary school for the meeting. Emotions ran so high that night John had little opportunity to present the church's plans. He spent most of his time denying rumors from angry residents who feared the loss of money from declining real estate values if Rock Church moved in.

"This is going to wreck our neighborhood," a gray-headed woman said tearfully. "It won't be a decent place to live!"

"You know what I wish, Mr. Gimenez," one man said angrily, "I wish you'd go to hell and build your church there."

John's pulse quickened, perspiration dripped from his forehead. "I'm sorry, sir, but God's church can't go

to hell," he answered firmly. "Your church might go to
hell — but not God's."

The man, hot and red-faced, started to reply, then
sat down. The crowd's disposition grew nastier.

John stood up and faced the people. "Folks," he
said, addressing the crowd with as much sincerity as
he could muster, "I'd like to say something to you all.
Today is my wedding anniversary and I came here
because you asked me. I've tried to answer all the
questions I can, but I'm leaving now."

People sat stunned at John's words.

"Whether you want it or not, God said to build the
church on that property," he continued, "and that's
where it's gonna be built."

Taking Anne's hand, they walked out.

Several weeks passed. The Planning Commission
gave Rock Church a top-to-bottom examination.
Then, it dropped a bombshell. Its report recom-
mended three restrictions be added to the use permit:
 • the church could not be used as a rehabilitation
   center;
 • the church could not be used to house persons;
 • and there could be no busing of persons to the
   church from rehabilitation centers or any other
   facilities.

Rock Church had to accept all three restrictions if it
wanted the use permit. Reluctant at first, John finally agreed.

Next, the permit went before the entire city council. A number of neighborhood residents, including
their highly vocal spokesman, attended the meeting.

"The reason we oppose this church being located
here is because John Gimenez wears two hats," the

stocky, cigar-chomping man stated. "He's a preacher and a drug rehabilitation worker. Wherever he goes, drug addicts come ... people who aren't desirable always show up. We feel he'd end up with a drug rehabilitation program there."

Mayor Rhodes spoke up. "When I was a kid, we were brought up to believe the church was the place for people who were in need or any trouble. In effect, the church was a rehabilitation place. I, for one, don't see anything wrong with the church doing the work of rehabilitation. It seems to me — that's the church's job."

Several people applauded the mayor's words. He gaveled them quiet.

"But, our real estate will go down," the neighborhood spokesman whined.

"Mr. Gimenez, what are you going to build there?" Mayor Rhodes asked.

John stood to his feet. "Sir, from the beginning, I've said we're going to build a church ... that's all. No one is going to sleep there or stay overnight."

"Then, you're not going to build a rehabilitation center?" another councilman questioned.

"No, sir," John responded, shaking his head.

"What is the use permit for?" the mayor inquired.

"A church," the city clerk said, looking over the report.

Several councilmen shifted and twisted in their chairs. "What are we arguing for?" a councilman muttered. "Why don't we go ahead and vote approval of the thing?"

Yet, one lone councilman held out for including the Planning Commission's restrictions. The situation looked stalemated. Then, John Jordan, an Episcopal priest, asked to be heard.

"Those limitations you've placed on Rock Church are illegal in my view," he announced. "I don't believe you can put limitations on a church as to how it will operate, or if it can bus people to its services. That's a violation of their constitutional rights."

The council chamber grew hushed.

"If you do that to them, you'll have to apply the same rules to me," he continued. "I counsel drug addicts ... I counsel alcoholics. You'll have to apply those rules to every church in Tidewater and you may wind up with a court case on your hands."

The air was tense.

"I move we strike all limitations from the permit," a councilman suggested, breaking the silence.

The vote passed 9-2. Next, they voted on the permit itself. The vote was 10-1. Rock Church now had its permit for using the land.

Valuable time had been lost through the struggle. More than three months passed from the time a contract was signed until a spade broke the ground. And all of that had taken the whole church praying and fasting!

John quickly hired a bulldozer for clearing and grading the land, followed by concrete laborers who began laying a $10,000 slab for the foundation. Within days, the lawyer who was to handle the property settlement telephoned.

"Mr. Gimenez, what in the world are you doing on that land?" he asked nervously.

"We're putting down a slab," John responded. "Winter's coming."

"You can't do that," the lawyer said excitedly. "You haven't closed on the contract. It's not your land yet. That kind of thing is against the law. You're actually building on somebody else's property."

"Well, I gave you $5,000 — all the money the church had — and you didn't give it back so I figured the deal was going through," John said innocently.

"It hasn't stopped ... that's for sure."

"My situation's like this," John explained. "We're already into late October. Winter weather will be here soon and I've got to finish this concrete work for the slab. These workers will be finished in a couple of days."

"I'll rush the closing date and maybe we can get this thing finalized without any further complications," the lawyer suggested. "But please, don't do any more work after the slab's finished!"

The contract settlement closed without any further problems. John's only immediate concern was construction money. The church's plans called for a 450-seat auditorium, six classrooms, a nursery, prayer room and fellowship hall. After paying for the concrete slab, the church coffers didn't have a dime left for a single brick.

At first, John thought the best way to handle the construction cost was borrow the money from a bank. Surely a construction loan wouldn't be difficult to obtain ... or would it? His first trip to a bank found him seated at the desk of a very efficient vice president. A pencil-thin mustache and a flower in his lapel highlighted the bank officer's appearance. "And what can we do for you today?" he asked.

"I need about $50,000 to $100,000 to build a

church," John announced, taking a seat.

The bank officer rubbed his chin and picked a few pieces of lint from his dark blue suit. "What's your collateral right now?"

"Uh," John thought for a minute. "I guess we don't have any."

"No collateral, huh?"

"That's right."

"Well, what's your background?" the man questioned. "Where did you go to school? And what about your credit history. Did you bring a financial statement with you?"

"Whew ... that's a lot to answer," John smiled. "I only got passed to the fifth grade, then I was kicked out of school for starting a fire. I never went back after that."

"Hmmm," the man muttered.

"I was a heroin addict for sixteen years in New York and I guess I don't have any credit references to speak of. My wife might have some."

"No credit and you're an ex-addict," the bank officer mumbled.

"Yeah, but Jesus Christ changed me," John enthused. "Let me tell you what God did in my life ..." By the time John finished his testimony, the banker wasn't about to loan him or Rock Church any money. A door had been tightly shut.

That troubled John initially but then the Lord spoke one day while he was in prayer. *"You'll not borrow from man. This building will be a miracle and a testimony to My grace. It will be totally paid for when you move in."*

Later, he shared the words with Anne. "Honey, God

said something to me and I'm not really sure I understand it."

"What'd He say?" she asked interestedly.

"He said this new building was going to be debt free
when we move in," he answered.

"That's going to be a novel approach," she remarked. "Most churches have to borrow and sell
bonds."

"I know," John admitted, "but that's what the Lord
said."

John still didn't understand the Lord's words.
Then, a few days passed and more understanding
came. The Lord impressed him that the church's pastors should be "an example for the flock." John knew
what that meant. Royalties on his first book had been
paid recently. The Gimenezes had saved about
$2,000.

"I want you to take the first step of sacrifice," the
Lord impressed upon him.

In turn, he went to Anne and mentioned what the
Lord had said. "God hasn't said anything to me about
emptying out our bank account," she retorted.

John's old nature would have called for him to
ignore her and do whatever he wanted. But he knew
better. "Honey, I know God told me," he said softly.
"I'm gonna pray that the Lord will just speak to you."

In a few days, Anne spoke up. "Sweetheart, you
were right. Let's empty out the account."

And that's exactly what the Gimenezes did. They
made the first step as the church's pastors. It quickly
became another principle they adopted. They would
never ask their people to take a step which they
themselves did not take first.

John forged ahead with the building effort just as if
the church had a bank account bulging with money.
Except for highly specialized sub-contracting jobs,
church members did all the construction work. That
included John donning a tattered pair of jeans and
digging ditches.

The first month's bills came to $7,500. When John
placed them together in a folder, he noticed how
heavy they felt. A sinking feeling grew in the pit of
his stomach. "Look at this stack of bills," he groaned
to Anne, "and we don't have $200 in the bank."

She just shook her head.

"But the Word of the Lord has been spoken," John
reminded himself. "The building will be debt free
when we move in."

The following Sunday the Gimenezes were dress-
ing for church when the Lord spoke again to John. He
immediately turned to Anne who was brushing her
hair. "Honey, God just spoke and said He'd give us a
miracle today. The money's in the church. The people
will respond and the bills are gonna be paid."

"Well, you're preaching today so that means I'm
taking up the offering," she said apprehensively.

"Yeah, but don't worry," he assured her. "God's
gonna move."

Anne was quiet for a few minutes. "I've raised a few
offerings in my day and I'm good for a few hundred
dollars — maybe even a thousand or two. But I've
never even thought about raising that kind of money.
You're talking about $7,500. I don't know about that
kind of money."

"Honey, God's gonna do it," he answered. "He said
He would do it."

As planned, Anne led the morning song service. Then, she bravely announced, "Brother John says that God spoke to him that we're going to raise a $7,500 offering to pay our bills for the building." She stopped, took a deep breath and continued. "John's faith is great but we've got to pay these bills tomor row, folks. We've got to have the money then."

The offering was collected and totaled. It came to about $2,500. "Well, I-I-I-I'm not going to push any further," Anne said anxiously. "We'll just close now. If any of you later feel ..."

John jumped up. "Wait a minute, honey," he said, walking to the pulpit. Anne handed him the microphone and sat down.

"Folks, God told me this morning," he said firmly, "and I know He told me that the bills would be paid. He said there would be enough money here to pay those bills. Somebody go back to my office and get out that folder of bills."

Hazel Sasser returned with the stack. "These are the bills that have been incurred by the church," John announced. "Now these are God's bills and God spoke to my heart. This is what we're going to do. We're going to worship the Lord. Will you worship with me?"

John held the bills in the air and began to walk back and forth across the platform. "Glory, hallelujah! Praise you, Lord!" For several minutes, he did that — waving the bills over his head and singing praises to God. Shortly, a few voices joined his. A spirit of praise began filling the room. More voices joined John's ... and more.

"I'll give a thousand dollars," somebody shouted

from the back.

"Hallelujah," John sang.

"I'll give $200," someone else yelled.

People were jumping up throughout the audience shouting and praising God. "I'll give, I'll give," they called out. Some were even running down the aisles with cash and checkbooks in hand.

Hands were raised toward heaven. Voices lifted up. The room was filled with the Glory of the Lord. When the offering was totaled, it came to over $8,000!

The church had crossed its own Red Sea. Everyone soon learned — when God gave His Word on a matter — it would be done. Anticipation rose in the hearts of the people as to what mighty acts God might accomplish in the future.

The first of each month, the bills were brought before the church. "Here they are," John always announced. "Let's praise the Lord for His goodness and His supply."

It never failed. God's supply always equaled Rock Church's need.

11

The Pillar Of Cloud Moves

Throughout the remainder of 1970 and into the early months of 1971, the building on Kempsville Road slowly took shape. It seemed to the Gimenezes the further the construction went, the bigger the crowd became. People gathered as the house of the Lord was built.

Friends had warned the Gimenezes that building programs kill preachers or give them ulcers — if nothing else. "If it doesn't wear you out physically, it'll be a drain on the people," one acquaintance predicted.

But that didn't happen. The blending of the Gimenez' ministry saw to that. While John took direction over the building's construction, the Lord gave Anne a spirit of faith in preaching the Word. The services never lagged. On the contrary, people continued to be saved and filled with the Holy Spirit while the finances flowed for the construction. Instead of being a difficult time as predicted, the Gimenezes found it one of the most exciting times of their lives.

The toughest part of the construction effort for

John wasn't raising the finances. That was easy compared to dealing with the Planning Commission. The staff member placed over Rock Church's building permits turned out to be the very man who had so strongly opposed the church locating there.

Most every day John found himself in the man's office. "What'd you want now?" the man always questioned, twisting his every-present cigar in his mouth.

"I need another use permit for the building," John explained, handing the man his plans.

No matter how the plans were presented, the man always had a pat answer — "You can't do it that way."

In one instance, Rock Church was required to give a half-acre right-of-way for a road dividing its property and the Presbyterian Church next door. "You know I feel like I'm back in New York," John responded about the property action.

"How's that?" the beady-eyed man asked.

John rubbed his chin. "I feel like I'm hanging out with a bunch of guys from New York again," he explained, half-smiling. "Those guys always carried pistols for sticking up people ... and I feel like I'm being stuck up."

Nearing the end of seven months of construction, John walked into the Planning Commission for his final permit before occupancy. His old nemesis walked out. "I'd like to invite you to come to our dedication," John announced, offering his hand.

The man looked at him and sneered. "Over my dead body," he lashed out. "I wouldn't go there if it was the last place on earth." And with that he walked away.

Dedication day came May 22, 1971. Some 800 people showed up for the opening services overflow-

ing the main sanctuary and requiring extra seats to
be set up. David Minor came down from Coudersport
to preach. He beamed proudly over the Gimenezes
like any proud father would have.

Just as the Lord had promised — when the doors
were opened — everything was paid for. That included construction materials and labor down to
the pews, carpets, chairs and piano. They were all
debt-free. It was a great time of celebration for
Rock Church.

A few diehards resisted the move. "This building's
big enough for our people," they whined, referring to
the Lens Avenue structure.

Some suggested, "God's blessing is here. It won't go
over there to Kempsville Road."

"I just don't care to go to church on that side of
town," one woman complained. "It'll just be terrible
in that new building."

The Gimenezes worked hard to dispel such an-
tiquated notions. "The blessing of God isn't on brick
and mortar," Anne told the church one morning. "It's
upon the people ... God's just giving us a bigger
sheepshed."

John joined her at the pulpit. "Folks, have no fear,"
he promised, "The blessing of the Lord will go with us.
Like the pillar of cloud hovered over the children of
Israel, God'll be there. I can guarantee it."

And sure enough, the blessing followed. The joyous, praise-filled services that characterized the services on Lens Avenue continued in high gear on
Kempsville Road. The spontaneity and freedom of
worship hit a new level. The people recognized the
location wasn't important. The crucial issue lay with

obeying God. The anointing of the Lord always followed such obedience.

Crowds jammed the new structure. Each Sunday, people flocked in to the church. Within a month or two following dedication, the sanctuary was overflowing. Freshly built walls were soon ripped out from the sides and back of the sanctuary. Then, the six classrooms, the social hall and the nursery were eliminated. Still more space was needed.

Stunned at the rapid growth, the Gimenezes weren't sure what to do next. Then, one of the construction crew approached John.

"Pastor, I think I can put a balcony in without much trouble," he volunteered. "It seems like that's the most logical place to expand next. Let me build it."

John thought for a few moments. "You're right," he said, snapping his fingers. "There's no place else to expand for right now. What do you need?"

"Just buy the material and I'll build it," the man offered.

"It's a deal," John agreed.

The balcony took shape rapidly but the extra space didn't last long. It was filled the first Sunday. Attendance had jumped to a thousand people in a few short months. Each Sunday, more new faces appeared.

Realizing they needed to live closer to the church, the Gimenezes bought a house at 316 Capot Road. One afternoon, John happened to be cutting the lawn when he noticed his next door neighbor watering some plants. "I think I'll greet this guy and maybe get in a word for the Lord," John thought to himself.

Turning off the lawn mower, John walked to the edge of the yard. "How're you doing," he asked.

"Oh, hello," the man responded, greeting John with a handshake.

"I just wanted to introduce myself," John said. "My name's Gimenez ... John Gimenez. My wife and I pastor the Rock Church down here on Kempsville Road."

The man, tall and muscular, smiled. "Oh, I know who you are," he answered.

"You do?"

"Yeah ... you see, I'm with the F.B.I. When I heard you'd bought a house next door, I wanted to check you out. I'd heard about your story of drug addiction and then your conversion. I wanted to see if it was all true."

"Hmmmmm," John mused.

"Let me show you something I found," the man announced, walking back into his house. John waited patiently wondering what the F.B.I. man had.

The man returned momentarily with a folder in hand. "Take a look at this," he said, handing it to John.

Opening the folder, John found his complete New York Police record including a mug shot taken from his last arrest — a "bust" for petty larceny. John hardly recognized the figure looking back from the mug shot. The bleary-eyed man had a disheveled appearance. The photo had the notation "9-3-62, N.Y.P.D." John remembered the arrest — for stealing some hypodermic needles. He'd spent six months in city jail as a result. It was his last arrest before he came to Christ in April 1963.

Tears ringed John's eyes as he looked back at the F.B.I. agent.

"I just wanted you to know I'm glad I found you

were telling the truth about your life," the agent said. "Your story's real."

"Yeah," John acknowledged."It's real—very real."

Since he'd come through a rehabilitation program, John somehow felt obligated to some phase of that ministry. Even though God had moved sovereignly to remove John from the Proclaim Center on Kempsville Road, he recognized a desperate need in the community for the work. He continually encountered troubled, drug-using youngsters.

During that time, realtors notified John about the availability of an old hunting lodge in Backbay near the North Carolina/Virginia border. The lodge, a rambling, wooden structure, and five acres reminded John of Mountaindale.

"This could be it," he thought.

Anne was reluctant to step out on the project, but she recognized John's heart-felt desire. "He always needs a challenge," she thought. "With his creative energies, this may be what he needs ... especially since the building program's ended.

John forged ahead, negotiating a price for the hunting lodge and raising a $5,000 down payment. Then, obstacles cropped up. Several people opposed the use permit at the Planning Commission meeting. The application was deferred for further study.

Meanwhile the church's growth continued. One Sunday as they were leaving the church, Anne looked up. She saw a low, two-story building coming from the side of the present sanctuary. She rubbed her eyes hardly believing what she'd seen.

"Oh, John," she enthused, "I know what we're going to do next."

"What do you mean next?" he asked, wheeling the car into the road.

"I just saw a two-story, flat roof building ... almost like in a vision. It'll be the education building and will come directly from the back of the sanctuary."

"Humph," John mumbled, not being particularly impressed with his visionary wife's words.

His attention focused on the Backbay project, John couldn't hear Anne's words. The following Tuesday night, he was ministering elsewhere so Anne had the service. She told the people about her vision. "I don't know if this was something like Daniel experienced or not," she declared, "but I know I saw it — just as plain as day."

Instead of groaning at the prospect of more construction, the crowd exploded in applause. They stood shouting, singing and praising God. "We're ready for more," several yelled.

After the service, a contractor in the church walked up. "Tell John when you get home that he's already got 10% of the new building paid for," he offered.

Anne grinned. "What do you mean?"

"Tell him that I'll handle all the electrical work — installation and supplies — and I'll donate it all *free*."

"Praise God," Anne shouted. "I'm sure he'll want to hear that."

When she returned home, Anne told John what had happened. "That's interesting, honey," he allowed, "but I'd like to wait and see what happens with the Backbay property."

"Okay, Anne said reluctantly. "You go ahead."

The Backbay property issue had been headline
news in the papers. Area residents opposed a drug
work being located there. Land speculators had also
hired a prominent attorney to resist John's efforts.
The Planning Commission's second meeting to consider the permit was a week away. John gathered several people to pray over the matter.

Driving to the old hunting lodge, they walked
throughout the building praying in the Spirit, they
met back in the living room. "Let's unite in prayer,"
John suggested. The seven people stood in a circle
joining hands.

As they prayed and praised, a prophetic word came
through John. Then he gave the interpretation. *"You
shall no longer be involved in rehabilitation, but you
shall be involved in discipleship training. You shall
give your time and attention to a training effort and
it will be called the New Jerusalem School of
Discipleship."*

Stunned, John could hardly believe the words. Yet
inwardly, he felt God had spoken.

The Planning Commission meeting lay a day or so
away. Newspaper stories predicted a court battle —
even if John received a use permit. Before the meeting came off, John telephoned the church's attorney.
"Call off the permit," he instructed. "I think God's
given us other marching orders."

Even John's withdrawal of the permit made head-
lines. "We're not here to cause problems for the community," John announced. "We're here to help. Tidewater has a drug problem — without question. But
God has a lot of ways in solving the situation. He
can do it — with or without a rehabilitation house

in Backbay."

Several area newspapers editorially supported John. They said it was tragic financial interests over-rode the public's concern for helping drug users. Some even encouraged John to look elsewhere for a loca-tion. But he knew better and turned himself to the educational building.

Gathering the church's leadership, the Gimenezes discussed the building and parking situation. Ironi-cally, when everything was finalized, the education building ended up exactly in the spot where Anne had seen it in her vision.

"I won't say I told you so," she promised John.

"Please don't," he laughed.

Once again, funds were raised from general offer-ings for the construction project. A few times, pledges were taken. During one such pledge time, a story that captures the uniqueness of Rock Church unfolded. Berta Jones, an eccentric, opinionated woman, ap-proached John after service one night. "Pastor, I want a word with you," she said sternly.

"Yes, indeed," he replied.

"I know God brought me to this church," she began. "But I can't stand these long-haired hippies you've got coming around here. I don't believe that's God."

"Why not?" John questioned.

She unfurled her Bible and thumbed to I Corin-thians 11:14. *"Doth not even nature itself teach you,"* she read, *"that, if a man have long hair, it is a shame unto him?"*

She paused and looked up at John. "Well, that's what the Word says," she announced confidently. "What're you going to do about it?"

"Sister, I'm doing everything I possibly can," he answered softly.

"What's that?" she probed.

"I'm letting them come here," he said, "and I'm letting the Holy Spirit deal with them. I feel God will take care of them."

Her face grew taunt as John spoke. The lines around her mouth hardened. Her eyes grew steely.

"It also says in the Scripture that we don't carry these things to a point of contention," he observed. "God will handle all of this. We just have to leave it up to Him."

"The devil you say ..." Berta replied, walking off in a huff. John groaned inwardly, knowing he'd probably lost her as a member, a tithe-paying one at that.

A few days later in the Sunday morning service, pledges were being received for the education building. Vinny Losciale, a young man with long hair, ragged beard and faded overalls, raised his hand. "I'll give a thousand dollars," he pledged.

John thought to himself, "That guy doesn't have a thousand dollars. Who is that hippie anyway? I know the devil's trying to mess up this meeting."

Vinny's friend, Cush Dobbs, who dressed enough alike to be a twin, raised his hand next. "I'll give eight hundred dollars," he volunteered.

Under his breath, John muttered, "In Jesus name, I rebuke you, devil." He *knew* the enemy was out to spoil the meeting.

Within days, the two guys paid their pledges. They had a prosperous carpentry business and deeply loved the Lord. John praised God that the people of Rock Church — he and Anne included — were being taught to love instead of judging. Vinny and Cush became a source of great blessing to many.

The new educational wing was constructed in nine months. Just like the sanctuary, it was built by the hands of the people and was debt free when occupied. Over $170,000 had been donated to pay for construction costs. About $50,000 was leftover for other projects. The Gimenezes were continually astounded at God's blessing. Could there be more?

12

"The Witch of Kempsville"

Rock Church had been located in its ever-expanding quarters on Kempsville Road for almost three years when Anne came to church early one night. The sanctuary was quiet, lights dimmed. She went to the altar for prayer and as she did the Spirit of the Lord upon her. Tears flowed.

"Daughter, you have withheld yourself from this people ... and in so doing you have deprived Me of using you as I desire," the Lord whispered. *"You must accept yourself as one of the pastors of this place. The day you do that the people will accept it ... and in so doing I will be glorified in your life."*

Anne knew the truth of what God spoke to her heart. "Yes, Lord," she acknowledged tearfully. "I'll obey You."

During the service that night, Anne waited only briefly before sharing her fresh experience. "I've got a confession to make and probably an apology too," she began, tears glistening in her eyes. "It's kinda hard to admit that you haven't accepted the full responsibility God's given you."

The people grew still, sensing the importance of

the moment.

"We've been here four years — going on five — and I've always said John's the pastor and I'm an evangelist ... I'll just preach when I'm supposed to. But God has spoken to me that I've allowed myself to be intimidated by people in this area."

Her voice quavered, "I-I-I." She stopped briefly and wiped her eyes. "Lord, bless her," someone encouraged.

"I-I-I've been so afraid they'd say John was henpecked," she continued, still dabbing her eyes with a wet, twisted handkerchief. "I've been concerned I'd unknowingly put him in a bad light. It's been a great struggle for me. Sometimes I haven't known what to do."

"Yes," several responded.

"I feel like I've cheated you by withholding myself from God's call here," she said plaintively. "But I just want you to know — from this day on — I'm accepting the job God's given me as one of this church's pastors."

Many stood and applauded her words. A few had sensed her struggle. They knew her life hadn't been easy the last several years — suffering a miscarriage, then giving birth at 37, and now trying to raise a child and keep up with an ever-growing church ... not to mention the normal slings-and-arrows of pastoring. They wept with Anne grasping the cry of her heart to serve God within her calling.

Anne could not have known what lay ahead by publicly agreeing to the Word of the Lord. Persecution — fueled by vicious and unfounded rumors — followed. Problems over her ministry had risen before. Orange, Texas, and Newport News were prime examples. The test that lay ahead would be as severe as Anne or John had ever known.

It started simply enough with various members approaching the Gimenezes with questions about what Rock Church believed. Often someone walked up after service with a troubled look on their face.

"Do you have a problem?" Anne would often ask.

"Yeah, but I'm not sure how to put it ... it's about *you*."

"Well, just say it out loud so I can at least try to clear up the situation."

"Sister Anne, I know you're of the Lord and you feed me," the person would say, "but my friends are saying I'm in error because one of the pastors here is a woman."

"Oh, I see."

"They're telling me I'm wrong and you're wrong too according to the Bible. Does the Bible say a woman isn't supposed to teach?"

Anne or John always answered the questions as best they could. Yet one answered question seemed to spawn another. And another. At times, they wondered if their visibility in Tidewater hadn't caused some of their problems. Since their earliest days on Lens Avenue, they had had a weekly program on television as well as radio.

But rumors abounded. Once John heard a local pastor was passing rumors about the Gimenezes and Rock Church. "Brother, I'm calling to check out something," he told the pastor by telephone.

"Sure — go ahead," the man responded.

"I've had several people tell me lately they heard you saying the pastors at Rock Church didn't believe in the second coming of Jesus or even in the blood of Jesus."

"W-W-W-W-ell," the pastor stammered. "That's what I understood."

"Let me ask you a question," John said seriously. "Have you ever been to Rock Church?"

"No."

"Have you ever personally heard me or my wife say we didn't believe in the second coming or in the blood of Jesus?" John bore down.

"No."

"Then, why're you going around saying that's what we believe?" he asked incredulously. "Don't you think that's unwise to be speaking about fellow ministers that way?"

The preacher's temper flared. "I just want to know one thing," he lashed out. "What're you doing with all those people over there."

"Ohhh, I see," John responded. "I see where you're coming from now."

"Yeah, that's right," the man answered. "Tell me."

"Brother, I'll be happy to tell you," he said sincerely. "We're taking care of the flock God's given us. We're feeding them. That's all."

"Humph," the preacher snorted, hanging up.

On another occasion, several local ministers objected to a speaker scheduled at Rock Church. The speaker, Bill Barton was known to hold some controversial views on scripture. John telephoned several responsible preachers concerning Barton, but no one had any clear-cut evidence against the man. On that basis, John decided to go ahead with the planned services. A deacons' meeting was called to finalize the matter.

"What're we going to do?" someone asked.

"Why don't we go along just this once," another suggested. "Let's cancel Barton."

John interrupted. "We can do that ... but what if cancelling Barton shows people they can dictate matters within Rock Church. What if next somebody suggests that Sister Anne quits preaching? What do we do then?"

No one seemingly had answers for that.

Several local ministers broke fellowship with John over the Barton issue. He frequently received word that most local preachers didn't mind him personally. They were bothered by Anne's ministry more so than anything else. In face, some suggested *she* was the source of false doctrine coming out of Rock Church. Such remarks grieved John.

The struggle over Anne's right to preach even touched personal relationships outside Tidewater. The Gimenezes had a good friend in John Paxton, who had succeeded his dad, Ned, as pastor of a full gospel church in Pennsylvania. Paxton, a tall, ruggedly handsome preacher, had ministered a number of times at Rock Church and was always favorably received.

The Gimenez' relationship with Paxton had been warm and close. He had never shown signs of personal prejudice toward women in the ministry. Yet, rumors slowly filtered back that his doctrinal position was changing. John wondered if the change could be due to Paxton's association with some noted charismatic Bible teachers who held similar views.

During a trip to Atlanta, John bumped into Paxton

attending the same conference. "We've got a few minutes between sessions," John mentioned. "Care for
some coffee?"

"Sure," Paxton agreed.

They walked leisurely into the bustling, hotel coffeeshop and found a convenient booth in the back.
"It'll be quiet here," John suggested.

"Yeah."

The two preachers chatted innocently over their
coffee. Then, Paxton said, "I'd like for you and
Anne to come up for a conference we're planning
in the fall."

"We'll try to keep the dates open," John promised,
sipping his coffee. "What'd you have in mind?"

"Naturally I'd like you to preach," Paxton
suggested, "but, uh..."

John waited as his friend seemingly searched for
the words. "Is there more?" he asked.

"Yeah — sorta," Paxton hedged apologetically. "We
don't allow women to minister in our church at all."

"Ohhhh," John responded. "We've heard something
about that."

He nodded. "Yeah, I'm sorry but that's just the way
I feel."

"Okay, brother, if that's your position," John said
simply. "We'll respect that."

Paxton drew an anxious breath. "I hope this won't
be a problem between us," he offered.

John smiled. "Brother, it's not my problem," he said
seriously. "It's *your* problem ... and I think you're
going to have trouble with it."

"Trouble — why's that?"

"It's the simple fact you minister in churches pastored by women," John answered, "and sooner or later they're gonna get wise to you."

Paxton didn't reply; instead he looked at his watch. "Time for the afternoon session," he announced, "I'd better get going."

John walked out of the coffeeshop while his friend rushed off to lead a teaching session. He wondered if his friend understood the double-mindedness of his position — preaching in churches pastored by women all the while being opposed to a woman in the ministry. "Is he sincere or just doing it for money?" John asked himself.

Several months passed. Then Paxton wrote an article in a national magazine detailing his position on women in the ministry. He was scheduled for an anniversary convention at Rock Church within several weeks. John read the article, then telephoned his friend.

"Brother, I just wanted to be fully sure about your position on women ministering in the church," John announced.

"I've pretty much put it all into that article," Paxton said.

"In that case, I'm going to be forced into cancelling you for our convention."

"What — cancel me — why?"

"It was okay when you held beliefs like that within the four walls of your own church," John explained. "But you've now written an article in a national magazine. Your position's known all over the country. And that position is totally opposed to what Rock Church has been built upon — Anne's and my ministry flowing together. I'd be crazy to let you come here and preach now."

"But, I..." he started to say.

"I just couldn't allow you to come," John interrupted. "I love you but I've got a responsibility to my
church. Your coming would bring confusion among
our people and that's not fair to them. I'm sorry —
real sorry."

The Gimenezes hurt privately over the situation
with Paxton. They prayed for him to come out of ex-
treme and back into a balanced ministry. Instead, the
opposite happened. Within a year or so, Paxton di-
vorced his wife and left the ministry. The Gimenezes
wondered if there was any connection between Paxton's views of women in the ministry and his marital
situation. Most likely they would never know.

The issue still loomed ever present before Anne. It
wasn't unusual for an earnest, young man to rush up
to the platform right after the morning service. "This
is my first time at Rock Church," he'd say invariably,
"and there's a scripture I'd like for you to explain — if
you can."

At times, the young man would thumb his Bible
unable to even locate the scripture. He simply knew it
was in the back.

"Try 1 Corinthians 14, verses 34-35," Anne would
suggest.

"Yeah, that's what I was looking for," he'd usually
reply, while hurriedly turning there.

Anne then would read the scripture. *"Let your
women keep silence in the churches: for it is not per-
mitted unto them to speak; but they are commanded to
be under obedience, as also saith the law. And if they
will learn anything, let them ask their husbands at*

home: for it is a shame for women to speak in the church."

The young man would usually nod at this point. "That's the scripture. Can you explain it?"

"First of all, chapter 14 is teaching church discipline and isn't teaching qualifications for ministry," Anne would begin. "You also need to realize in those days the custom was for the men to sit on one side of the church and the women the other.

"Now consider the fact that during a meeting, the wives were calling back and forth to their husbands asking questions. They were disrupting the service. Thus, Paul declared, 'If you want to know something, don't ask during the service, wait until you get home'."

Anne's positive answers seemed to unnerve the questioners as much as anything else. They seemed to struggle between the simplicity of her explanation and the severity of what they'd heard the scripture meant.

Although she had gained understanding for the scripture in 1 Corinthians 14, Anne had yet to find any answers for 1 Timothy 2:11-13. It read: *"Let the woman learn in silence with all subjection. But I suffer not a woman to teach, nor to unsurp authority over the man, but to be in silence. For Adam was first formed, then Eve."*

For months, she prayed over the scripture. Then, the Holy Spirit impressed her the scripture referred to a husband and wife's relationship. Thus, Paul had written, "I suffer not a woman to teach or to take authority *over her husband* but to be in silence and to be in subjection."

Several weeks later, well-known Bible teacher and author, Judson Cornwall, came to the church. Over lunch, Anne posed the question. "Judson, you've studied the scripture as thoroughly as anyone I know. I've taught that 1 Timothy 2:11-13 teaches the husband/wife relationship. What's your understanding about that?"

He smiled, picked up his Bible and pulled a sheet of paper from it. Anne took the paper and read. The verses from Timothy were typed three times with interpretations from three different theologians — Knox, Young, Williams. Each man's exegesis bore out Anne's understanding. The scripture covered a husband and wife's relationship — nothing more.

Even though Anne, as well as John, had a thorough grasp of scripture, it didn't stop the verbal brickbats from coming. One radio preacher often referred to a mysterious woman preacher he called "the witch of Kempsville." The woman, according to him, was laboring in deep, dark heresy. Anne had no doubt in her mind who the man was speaking about.

At times when rumors ran hot and heavy, even close friends made odd suggestions. "I've got to talk with you a few minutes," Chris Chase said, grabbing Anne as she and John walked into a Full Gospel Businessmen's meeting one evening.

"Yeah, sure," Anne agreed.

John strolled into the meeting while Anne turned to her friend. "What's up?" she asked.

"I've just heard about all the stuff you've been going through and all the preachers against you," Chris said sympathetically.

"It's been hard," Anne admitted, "but we'll make it."

"For the sake of unity in the body of Christ, why don't you just quit preaching for a while?" she questioned seriously. "Or maybe just withdraw from the ministry."

Anne couldn't believe her friend's suggestion. "I don't fear these men who've opposed me — or even what they can do," she replied simply. "They didn't put me in the ministry and it's a cinch they can't take me out."

John suffered equally under the load — maybe more. People badgered him, writing unsigned notes and making anonymous phone calls. At times, the pressure, together with the normal run of problems for a thousand-member congregation, created enormous stress. He and Anne continually made "mental" plans to escape. They figured on returning to evangelistic work. Surely they would be happier back on the road.

After a particularly rugged day, the Gimenezes prepared early for bed. They were both tired, drained. "I know this is as rough on you as it is me," Anne suggested, smoothing back the bed covers. "If you want me to withdraw for a while, I'm willing."

John looked at her, startled at such a comment. "Anne, you had a ministry when I met you. Before I'd ever destroy what God's done in your life, I'd get away from you."

Anne lay down on the bed and slowly pulled up the covers. She was quiet.

"I can handle what they've said about me if that's bothering you," John continued. "I just want you to do what God's called you to do."

"Maybe we can go back to evangelistic work once

we find somebody to replace us here," she pondered, turning off the bed lamp.

"Maybe," he allowed in the darkness.

Yet the Lord cut off any such hasty exits.

Several weeks later, the Gimenezes traveled to Detroit for a convention at Bethesda Missionary Temple. Each morning, they sat on the platform with some 50 ministers. "I'd like to change sides this morning," Anne said when they arrived. "Let's sit on the left instead of the right."

"Sure," John agreed, as they maneuvered to the left side of the pulpit.

"Oh, look," Anne said. "There's seats on the second row behind Jim Beall and Brother Schoch. Let's sit there."

The meeting followed shortly and then David Schoch, pastor of Bethany Chapel in Long Beach, rose to preach. "Last night while I was sleeping, the Lord awoke me and gave me a message for the Gimenezes," he began. "In turn, I woke up the brother who was sleeping in my room. Is that right, Brother Smith?"

"Yes, it is," came a reply.

"I told the brother I'd give the message this morning if the Lord allowed Brother and Sister Gimenez to sit behind me," he continued, "and that's what happened."

People turned looking for the Gimenezes. They were seated exactly where Schoch predicted — behind him.

Pointing a finger at John and Anne, he prophesied forcefully, *"Thus saith the Lord to his servants, the Gimenezes, you have thought to leave the place where you are. You have brought it to birth though and I re-*

quire that you bring it to maturity. You think that you've seen the ultimate, but you have not scratched the surface of what I am going to do there."

"Whew, thank You, Lord," Anne whispered.

"Praise You, Lord," John sang.

Schoch's prophetic message ended any ideas of slipping out the back door of Rock Church. No matter how difficult the situation became, the Gimenezes had been constrained — in an unforgettable fashion — to stay. The rumors, reactions and problems naturally didn't cease overnight. They ebbed and flowed like the changing tide.

The Gimenezes simply vowed between themselves to ignore it all and do what God had called them *together* to do. In simple obedience, they found great peace. Nothing could be more satisfying.

13

Raising Up The Staff

Without a doubt, Hazel Sasser had become a valuable asset to Rock Church. As the church's first member, she had also functioned as pianist and secretary for several years. Her full attention was now devoted to the church's growing music ministry which included a 50-voice choir and a small band.

A strong-willed, multi-talented woman, Hazel's personality and temperament were much like John's. Frequently, they locked "verbal" horns like battering mountain rams whenever she openly expressed herself. At times, she talked *too* openly.

During one of those heated conversations, John said simply, "I can't take it anymore ... you're fired."

At first, Hazel thought this was like all the other times they'd disagreed. She recalled John had said she was fired on some of those occasions too. But this time, it was for real.

John called a meeting of the church choir. "God has called Sister Anne and myself as the church's pastors," he explained, "and there's been some differences with Hazel. We've talked but we can't seem to work out matters ... so for the time being she will not be choir director."

Several choir members dropped out as a result of Hazel's departure from the church's music ministry. Rumors floated around about the situation. John agonized over the problem but he felt his hands were tied. No one was indispensable to the church's staff — not even he or Anne.

At times, Hazel came to the service and sat on the front row shooting daggers with her eyes at John. Whenever he walked to the pulpit, she always stood up and walked out. People were distracted.

Some six months after the situation occurred, John encountered Hazel at a Tidewater funeral home. As it turned out, he had been requested to preach the funeral while she was to sing. Neither knew the other would be there. In a small room outside the mortuary's chapel, John saw her sitting beside the door, looking over some sheet music.

He walked to her. "Hazel ... Hazel," he said softly.

She turned her face to the wall and buried her attention in the sheet music.

"Hazel, can't we be friends?" John asked gently.

She wheeled, eyes flaming. "I don't want you as a friend, John," she snapped. "I don't care to have anything to do with you."

The words cut like a plunging rapier. John's heart ached. "How could he do a funeral under such conditions?" he wondered to himself.

He started to walk away, then turned back. "Can we have prayer before we go out there?" he said, trying to soothe Hazel.

She shook her head firmly. "I don't need to pray," she fired back. "You're the one who needs prayer."

But God was dealing with Hazel. Months after the incident happened, she was in church one night when Charlotte Baker preached a stirring message on reconciliation. The Word of the Lord tugged at the strings of her heart. In tears, she ran to the altar.

Seeing her, John stepped from the platform to minister. Finishing the prayer, he looked her squarely in the eyes. "I love you, Hazel," he said sincerely.

Hazel *knew* his words were genuine, but she said nothing.

In the meantime, she had taken a secretarial job. She'd also been talking with other churches about directing their choirs. At the crossroads of decision, she walked into the restroom at work one afternoon and prayed fervently. "Lord, what shall I do? Where shall I go?"

The Word of the Lord came unmistakably. *"I don't want you to go anywhere. I've called you to minister at Rock Church. If you'll sit, I'll restore you."*

Hazel determined to obey God, returned to Rock Church and waited. In time, bitterness over the ordeal began to die. Heartfelt praise began to flow. The weight lifted from her spirit.

Fourteen months passed in all. John approached her one night following a service. "Would you like to have the choir back?" he asked simply. "I think God's done His work."

There was no hesitation. "Yes," she responded, knowing full well the miracle God had performed.

It was a critical time in the ministry of Rock Church. John had to face disciplining one of the church's most visible members. Not to mention the fact, she was the *only* member at one time. But as pastor, he was constrained to act as he did.

Hazel also had to learn her role in the church's ministry. She needed to recognize God hadn't called her to pastor. She had musical talents. Her ministry grew considerably more fruitful as she found her calling and rested in it.

As the Jesus Movement came on the scene in the late 1960s and early 1970s, the Gimenezes saw a need for the young converts to be taught the Bible. Rock Church's Bible School grew out of that need.

At the time, proficient Bible teachers were hard to find. Thus, the Gimenezes thought they'd found the right man in William McKinney, a tall, white-haired preacher, who had been in the ministry some 40 years. "God has sent me," he announced. He was quickly hired.

McKinney taught for several months before any problems surfaced. From time to time, students approached either John or Anne with questions about doctrine the outspoken preacher had taught. The Gimenezes wondered what kind of problem they had imported.

Then, Harvey Best, a young, serious Bible student, came to John. "I gotta know what the church believes," he said. "Brother McKinney's teaching that women have no place in the leadership of the church ... and this confuses me about your wife's role here."

"Ah-ha," John replied, understanding why others had brought questions. "That's not our position and we'll get it straightened out right now."

Calling McKinney to his office, John laid all the cards on the table. "I've heard you're teaching that a woman can't hold a position of authority in the church."

He nodded. "Sister Anne has a right to minister but she should not hold a leadership position," he offered.

"You understand that my wife and I are co-pastors here?" John questioned.

"Yeah."

"How can we minister together if you're saying one thing and we're saying another?" John asked. "The Bible says two can't walk together unless they be agreed."

"I know how you feel," McKinney suggested, "but that's how I see it."

The Gimenezes recognized two important lessons God was teaching them through people like McKinney. First, they needed to train up their own people for church jobs. And second, in order for the church to flow together, the people must be taught foundational principles for the Christian life.

As they sought the Lord and searched the scriptures, the Bible principles became obvious:

(1) the inspired Word of God, the virgin birth and salvation through the blood of Jesus; (2) water baptism; (3) baptism in the Holy Spirit; (4) gifts of the Spirit; (5) demon possession and Christians; (6) a woman's place in the church; (7) tithing; and (8) soul winning.

The principle of hiring Rock Church-trained people was proven first with John DeCarmo, who had been attending since the days on Lens Avenue. Little involved in the church at first, he was diagnosed as having cancer. Even after surgery, his life hung in the balance for weeks. The entire church united in prayer for him. Healing came gradually to DeCarmo who was unable to work for many months.

At a morning prayer meeting, John asked De-Carmo, "Please lead us in prayer."

As he prayed, the Word of the Lord came to John. *"You have been called to the ministry,"* he prophesied, laying hands upon DeCarmo, *"and you will minister the Word of God with great power and authority. You will be a mighty vessel in God's hands."*

Within months, DeCarmo's body was completely restored. Instead of returning to secular work, he resigned and joined the staff of Rock Church as an associate minister. DeCarmo's duties would vary like the Gimenezes. At times, he'd preach or lead singing. Other times during construction, he'd hammer and nail.

In the days ahead, the Gimenezes would see the beauty of their training principle paying off. "I used to see Proverbs 22:6 on training a child as just for kids," John told Anne one day. "But I'm seeing it in a new light now — like raising up ministers."

"Right," Anne acknowledged. "Remember that experience with Jake Johnson at Proclaim. He was trained some place else. Look what happened with him."

"Yeah," John remembered the painful experience with the tough-minded Johnson. He determined that Rock Church's staff would be different.

From time to time, people drove to Rock Church from locations outside Tidewater. They all seemed to share a common goal. "There needs to be a Rock Church where we live," many of them suggested. The Gimenezes were naturally reluctant. They had their hands full in pastoring the growing church on

Kempsville Road.

Several people were persistent though. A group from Nags Head, North Carolina, in particular. For several years, ten people or so drove round trip every Sunday — some 150 miles in all. "We'd really like to get a Rock Church down there," Fay Nelson frequently begged.

"I tell you what," Anne promised one day. "You get us a place to meet and we'll get something started."

"You've got a deal," Fay enthused.

Within a few days' time, Fay had found a restaurant meeting room complete with a platform and organ. It was ready made for mid-week services. The Nags Head group fanned out corraling about 50 people for the first service. The Gimenezes and several others went down initially. Then, others in the church shared in the new work.

The church grew rapidly. It became evident to the Gimenezes that God wanted to establish a Rock Church there. In time, they established a branch church with well over 100 members. It became the first of some 28 affiliate churches that would spring up in the Rock Church Fellowship.

The Bible School's director changed several times. Finally, Betty Forbes, who'd suggested the Lens Avenue location in the first place, became director. She joined Hazel Sasser and John DeCarmo as the church staff. Then came youth pastor Bart Pierce whose testimony is a story within itself.

Orphaned in his teenage years, Bart rebelled against society turning to a life of drugs and robbery. His reputation earned him the nickname "Black Bart" for his evil ways.

He and his wife, Coralee, stumbled into Rock
Church one Sunday morning. In spite of his clothes —
dirty tee-shirt, sneakers, jeans, shoulder-length hair
and beard, he was welcomed with open arms.

Cush Dobbs and Vinny Losicale, who had known
him in the drug scene around Virginia Beach, spotted
him in the crowd. "Hey, Bart, how long you known
Jesus?" they asked.

Bart was dumbfounded. He didn't know what they
were talking about. He just smiled. "Yeah, cool, man."

When he and his wife drove away from the church,
she remarked, "You know, when they had that altar
call I wanted to go up there."

"What?"

"I really wanted to go forward. There's a void in me,
an emptiness, that's just not getting filled. Maybe
this church thing will do it — maybe religion's the
answer."

Bart couldn't grasp what she was saying. "Maybe
she's planning to leave me," he thought to himself.

Several months slipped by. Then, one day, they
came back to Rock Church. This time Bart thought he
could handle the service better if he sat in the back of
the auditorium. "Ought to be safer there," he figured.

But when the altar call was given, the magnet of
the Holy Spirit shifted into overdrive. Bart was laboring under such heavy conviction he jumped out of his
seat and ran down the aisle to the altar. Amid tears of
repentance, he asked Jesus to come into his life and
make Himself real to him. When he stood up, Bart
saw that Coralee was at another altar. Serving Christ
would become a family affair for the Pierces.

14

The Round Building

Several women in the church had a burden for a Christian school. Classes for kindergarten and first grade were held temporarily, but the program seemed to fizzle. Interest lagged. For another year the idea of a Christian school lay dormant.

Then one Sunday morning during services the offering was being taken. Anne turned to John. "The reason we don't have a school is because we don't have the buses to bring the kids."

John looked surprised. "If that hadn't come out of your own mouth, I'd have never believed it. I know how you feel about the expense of a school, not to mention the buses."

The offering concluded; the music stopped. "How many of you want to know what I just said to John?" Anne asked, walking to the pulpit.

People clapped. "Yeah, tell us," several shouted.

"I just said the reason we don't have a school for our kids is we don't have the buses to bring them," she explained. "I told him I just saw three yellow school vans with 'Rock Church' written on the sides. I believe God wants us to have a school."

"Amen," people yelled.

"How much are those vans? Anne questioned, looking around for some knowledgeable person.

"I think they're about $5,000 each," John volunteered, walking up beside her.

"Great," Anne enthused. "I believe God wants us to have those vans to begin a Christian school. What do you folks say?"

Immediately, people were up and out of their seats. The altar began to fill with checks, cash and pledges. The donations came to $15,000 — enough for the three yellow vans. The following day they were ordered.

That was the spring of 1974. In the fall, the church opened the doors of Rock Christian Academy using the educational building as the school house. The academy would eventually have students from kindergarten through high school.

Within two years, Rock Church had outgrown every conceivable inch of available space. For over a year, two morning services had to be held to accommodate the growing numbers of people. It was time to build again.

Many times John walked into his office and found designs for auditoriums. The designs were usually accompanied by little notes saying, "God spoke to me that you should build it this way."

A builder in the church came offering suggestions as to how a structure could be erected. "I know how you can save all kinds of money," he promised. John still didn't feel impressed to take action.

Then someone remarked casually to John, "I just feel in my heart the building's gonna be round."

That agreed with John's spirit, but he wasn't positive. He didn't have a clear word of direction from the Lord. Neither did Anne — and that's what they had always operated on.

One muggy afternoon John was driving to the church. When he reached the property, the Holy Spirit came down upon him and he began speaking in tongues. It rolled over him. He piloted the car onto the parking lot which had a tall utility pole in the center.

To John, it seemed as if the Holy Spirit had laid hands upon him. Getting out of the car, he began walking rapidly around the utility pole, his hands in the air, speaking in tongues. For several minutes, John circled the pole.

Finally he stopped and walked toward the building. Only then did he notice a bus load of people had pulled onto the parking lot for a visit to the church. Several people smiled as John walked past the bus. They had evidently seen his strange antics in the parking lot.

"Praise God," John chuckled to himself.

He rushed into his office to call architect Ken Thompson. "It's round, Ken, it's round," he shouted. "The Lord just let me know the building should be round."

"Praise the Lord," Ken yelled. "I knew it would be. I'll have plans in your hands in a couple of days."

With the church's deacons and Anne agreeing, John gave the people God's direction in the project the next Sunday. A token building fund offering of $30,000 was taken. "Somebody go get a shovel," John announced with obvious delight.

Then, the Gimenezes and the entire congregation
— more than a thousand people in all — marched
promptly out the door and broke ground. The new
building was underway.

Problems cropped up right away. First, there had to
be public hearings on the construction permits. The
initial meeting turned into a forum for Kempsville
residents to rebut the ministry of Rock Church.

"I really don't understand what kind of building
they're going to put up there," said a neighborhood
resident who opposed the construction.

"Think of Scope Coliseum in your backyard," one of
the Planning Commission's members remarked.
"That's what they're talking about."

"Scope?" the resident puzzled, thinking of the
10,000-seat coliseum.

At that point, Betty Forbes' husband, Skeets, nor-
mally a quiet man, asked to be heard. "I thought this
committee was supposed to be impartial and render
impartial decisions," he said firmly. "But what I'm
hearing from some of the members shows me there's
no impartiality here. Anybody who makes a statement as I've just heard about Scope being in a backyard doesn't know what he's talking about. We're not
talking about anything that big."

Realizing the mistake, the committee chairman
asked for a temporary recess. When the meeting re-
sumed later, the tone was modified but the opposition
was still strong. After several weeks of wrangling,
the building's dimensions were shaved some 200 feet
before Rock Church received final approval.

Once that hurdle was cleared, construction started.

Soon giant, yellow bulldozers were scooping hugh mounds of earth from the lot and mammoth steel girders were rising from the foundation. Years before, John wondered how the church could ever use all five and a half acres. Each day when he drove to the property, he praised God for having provided it all.

As Anne would discover, John operated in unique realms of faith during the construction project. One morning she was stopped in the hallway outside John's office. "Wasn't it wonderful what Brother John did the other night?" a heavy-set, graying woman asked.

"What do you mean?" she replied.

"Oh, he pledged $10,000 to the building fund," the woman exclaimed.

At first, Anne was astounded, then it made her angry that John would pledge such an amount and never mention it. Turning to the woman, she said, "The crazy thing is God'll probably give it to him."

Later when she and John talked about the pledge, they agreed the donation would not be taken from their salaries. Two weeks passed. A letter arrived one day from a church where John had recently preached. "Here's something extra for helping in our building fund," the letter said. The "something" was a check for $1,000 made payable to John Gimenez.

"Here's the first one," he announced smiling.

"Aren't you glad too," Anne grinned.

Within seven months, the entire $10,000 pledge was paid — all from outside sources. During this time, it was not unusual for John to raise large sums of money for other church building programs. In fact, one church in Oregon received pledges totaling

$800,000 the day John shared the miracle of Rock Church's building program.

As had been done with the first sanctuary, Rock Church paid cash as the new building took shape. Each week, John presented the construction bills and took an offering. The collection always covered the bills.

That was fine when the debts stood $20,000 or $30,000. But one Sunday morning, the church needed over $100,000 the following week. The contractor would proceed no further with construction unless that amount was paid.

John gave the news to the church. "Folks, I've prayed and I feel God told me a hundred men would stand with me this morning and give a thousand dollars apiece ... and as the church's pastors, Anne and I are giving the first thousand."

With that, he took out his checkbook, wrote a check and laid it on the altar. A hush fell over the congregation.

"I know women are usually the givers but God told me the men would stand with me this morning," he continued. "We've got to have this money tomorrow. Now — we're going to sing and praise the Lord until the need is met. I want everybody to praise God with me."

With hands raised, John began worshiping and praising the Lord. The band fell in behind. The choir sang. Others worshiped. "Hallelujah to His Name ... Praise the Lord ... Glory to His Name ... Praise the Lord ..."

Slowly men stood and came down the aisles. Checks began filling up the altar. Men lined the front.

Yet, more came forward. When the altar call stopped, more than a hundred men stood across the front and down the aisles of the church. Everyone held hands as John led a concert of praise and worship for the Lord's provision.

Standing on the platform, Anne looked at some of the men pledging a thousand dollars. "There's no way in the world they'll be able to come up with that kind of money in a day or so," she thought.

But the money came. Construction never lagged. No one person would ever be able to take credit for the building — not John, Anne or anybody else. A sovereign move of God was responsible.

Since the new sanctuary would be round, the large platform area housing the 100-voice choir and orchestra was planned with a round-effect also. The Gimenezes were looking over the construction one afternoon to the staccato sounds of hammering and the rhythmic pull of sawing.

"I sure like the way the seating will be done." Anne volunteered, looking at the floor gracefully sloping toward the platform.

"Me too," John agreed.

They walked hand in hand, chatting with various laborers and absorbing a feel for the wide-opened auditorium. 'But that's something I don't like," John suddenly announced, releasing Anne's hand and walking off to the platform.

Steps were being constructed on either side of the platform. "I don't want those steps in that place," John said to several men who were nailing a wooden form in place.

"Why's that?" one of them asked. "That's what the

plans call for."

"Maybe so," John replied, "but I'm changing them."

"Why?" Anne chimed in.

"This church has been built by people," John explained to both Anne and the two men. "This is a big, fancy building but that isn't going to keep me away from the people. I can't minister to them unless I can reach them."

"You're right," Anne said, nodding her head.

"Give me some steps right in front of the pulpit," John instructed. "I want an open platform for the people to receive ministry from. Let's construct it that way."

"Sure," the workmen agreed.

Throughout the months of construction, the miracle-working power of God stood ever present. Prayer meetings were held each morning. Men saved at the church — Bart Pierce, Vinny Losciale, Cush Dobbs — used their able building skills. Butch Strange, who'd later joined the church staff, took nine months off from his secular job just to help.

Josiah Woodington, who'd donated the electrical work in the original sanctuary, gave electrical supplies and services worth $12,000 to the church. His labor included the huge overhead lights in the new sanctuary.

Continual miracles of provision and protection occurred. Once a construction worker fell from a scaffold and landed on his back three stories below. He sustained only a few scratches, nothing serious at all.

Dedication came in May of 1977 — seven years from Costa Dier's prophecy exhorting "arise and build for the thousands." The thousands were here now and they had donated more than two million dollars for the new sanctuary. Only $100,000 was owed as the church entered the new building. Within a few months, that debt was paid leaving the structure debt-free.

The Gimenezes expected a good crowd for dedication day. Sure enough, all 3,000 seats were filled and overflowing. Sunday after Sunday that happened. The church stayed consistently full. Even though the new building was twice the size of the original sanctuary, crowds continued jamming the place. In time, a second morning service would be needed to make room for all the people.

It was only after the months of construction ended that both John and Anne realized how bone-tired they were. The church gave them a love offering for a well-deserved vacation. Leaving Robin with Anne's parents who'd come for the dedication, they drove only as far as Myrtle Beach, S.C. They were simply too exhausted and fatigued to proceed further.

The next morning, Anne awoke early and sat staring as an orange sun rose out of the broad expanse of ocean. The morning was quiet, still. Anne was alone with her foreboding thoughts.

An hour later, John stirred. Anne was still sitting at the window. "What's up?" he asked drowsily.

"I've just been watching the sun come up," she said.

Rubbing his eyes, he looked for his watch. "How long you been up?"

"A good while — I've been waking up a lotta nights lately. I guess I'm just too tired to sleep."

"Huh? What're you talking about, darlin'?" he asked, puzzled at Anne's response.

"We haven't made *any* plans beyond building that new church," she allowed. "Now we'll have to pastor that big thing. I'm wondering if it'll destroy us."

"What do you mean?" he asked seriously, sitting up on the side of the bed.

"Robin and I didn't see much of you when we had 1,500 people. What'll happen with double that number?"

"Honey, there'll be time," he promised, walking over to her and massaging the back of her neck. "There'll be time."

"I hope so," she said wistfully. "I *really* hope so."

15

Hitting The Airwaves

About a month after entering the new sanctuary, a new Assemblies of God church was due for dedication in the Tidewater area. John was out of town, so Anne went out of courtesy to the pastor who'd attended Rock Church's recent dedication. As it turned out, Pat Robertson was the dedication speaker.

At the close of the meeting, Anne waited until the crowd had diminished around the ever-popular CBN founder. "Do you want to shake hands with one more little old lady?" she asked, extending her hand.

Pat smiled. "I'll do better than that," he enthused, "I'll give you a kiss." And with that, he leaned over and lightly kissed Anne on the cheek.

"Pat, what would it take to get you to come to Rock Church some Sunday night and speak?" Anne asked with a grin.

"Only a phone call," he answered.

"I'll see that you get it," she promised.

That Sunday night when she returned to church, she teased the crowd. "I'm never gonna wash this side of my face again. How many of you want to know why?"

Hands lifted throughout the auditorium.

"Pat Robertson kissed me on the cheek this afternoon," she announced, "and what's more he promised to come to Rock Church and preach."

Everybody applauded.

The next day when John returned home, Anne told him about her conversation with Pat. "He'll never have time to come ... he's so busy with CBN and everything," John predicted.

"Oh, yes, he promised," Anne said confidently.

In late July, Pat came for a Sunday night service. The building packed to the rafters producing the largest crowd to date in the new sanctuary. During the service, Pat reminisced about being sent to Tidewater. "It was a spiritual wasteland then," he said, "but God told me it would become a watering place."

Then he described the thrilling revival of 1965 which came to the area. "At the end of the week, I went to London and met John Gimenez who had a revival of his own going on among the addicts of Soho."

The people laughed and applauded as Pat remembered meeting the newly married Gimenezes in Bogota in late 1967, and then their first appearance on the "700 Club" the following year.

Pat's message on "The Christian's Sprritual Heritage" caught like wildfire among the thousands of people. A spiritual explosion rocked the crowd launching it out into sustained praise and worship.

At the close, John graciously thanked Pat for his stirring sermon. "We're so grateful for Brother Pat," he acknowledged. "There are many people in the ministry today because this man obeyed God in coming to Tidewater and starting CBN."

Later that night, the Gimenezes went to dinner with Pat. Over the meal, John said, "We've been off television because of our building program for about two years, but we'd like to go back on. Is there any chance of getting on CBN?"

Pat thought for a moment. "Do you want a local or national program?"

"What do you mean?" John asked.

"If you can give us a quality program, you can be on satellite all over the country," Pat suggested. "That reaches 15 million people or more."

John grinned thinking of the outreach. "Well, we want a program based in the church. One that shows the joy and worship in our services."

"Sounds good," Pat said.

"What would we need to do?" John questioned, sensing an opened door.

"Look," Pat offered. "You'll need special equipment which we could help you get. I'll just write to all my department heads and tell them to help you in anyway possible."

"Hallelujah," John responded.

Pat made good his promise. CBN's broadcasting pros were quickly made available to Rock Church. "This church is perfectly built for doing a television program," one of their engineers suggested.

"It wasn't built with that in mind," John said, "but I guess the Lord makes allowances for that. Huh?"

"Yeah," the man grinned.

Several people approached John before the televised services were scheduled to air. "Are you going to tone everything down now that you're going on T.V.?"

they asked.

"Not at all," John smiled. "In fact, we may even step them up a notch or so. I want people to see it like it is. They can praise and rejoice with us. That's what the church is all about."

On the first anniversary of the round building's dedication — May of 1978, "Rock Church Proclaims" hit the airwaves. Response was immediate. "When I see your program, I feel like I've been to church," one man wrote.

"I used to go to a church like yours," a letter acknowledged. "I didn't know there were any churches around like that today."

There were other letters too. Some carping about "women preachers," or about the upbeat 27-piece orchestra. But those letters were far in the minority.

In time, the Gimenezes would come to see the great blessing of the televised services. In one telecast alone, they were reaching more people than years of preaching could ever cover. Folks who'd counseled them years before to stay on the evangelistic field instead of stopping to pastor, would be astounded now to see the Gimenezes ministering to tens of thousands.

Since God had spoken to Anne about "the windows of heaven being open" over Rock Church, there had never been room enough to contain the people. The principle worked at Rock Church, the Gimenezes found, because they first gave out. Then, God returned. The return always proved larger. There was never room enough to hold it.

Every time the Gimenezes drove to church, they

passed a strip of 25 acres located on Kempsville Road. One day a for sale sign appeared on the property. "I gotta a feeling we ought to buy that," John suggested.

"Maybe so," Anne nodded.

Every visiting evangelist who came through town was given a tour of the property as John comtemplated the situation. On his way to a men's breakfast one morning, John drove past the property. Glancing at the strip, he found himself saying, "I claim it in Jesus' Name."

At the breakfast he shared his experience with the men. Afterwards, a man from the church walked up and gave $1,000 towards the property. "It's seed faith," he said.

A realtor had previously talked to John about the property. Calling the man, he announced, "I'd like to make an offer on that land ... I've got $1,000 to send with a contract."

"That's crazy," the realtor fumed. "That property is worth hundreds of thousands. They won't consider it with such a small binder. That's prime land. It'll be a miracle for that to happen."

John laughed. "Well, I believe in miracles ... so just send it in and let's leave the rest to God."

"Okay," the realtor agreed.

The property owners sent a hurried reply back: "We'll consider your offer, but only if you put $5,000 down."

John brought the matter before the church. Everyone agreed to proceed and a purchase price was negotiated. John's ever-creative mind went to work on how the church might use the property. He had a variety of ideas — retirement home, youth center, new church outreaches.

Months passed. Yet none of John's plans had taken shape beyond the planning stage. Christmas drew near.

The Gimenez' schedule was already pressure-packed. Counseling appointments and various meetings. The phone rang continually. Then they learned their television production schedule would have to be doubled during the month of December. Instead of one T.V. program a week, they did three. Anne felt the strain far more than John.

Many nights she stood in the wings waiting for the service to begin and fighting back tears. "Go out there and look like you're saved," she'd tell herself.

John noticed Anne's unusual tenseness, but he thought she was simply tired. She felt if she could just hold herself together until after Christmas, things would change for the New Year. But the T.V. production schedule and the demands of the ministry intensified the strain.

The Saturday before Christmas, Anne broke down and began to cry. She grew frightened when she could not control herself. John was bewildered, not knowing what to say or do. Robin ran to her room and locked the door. She had never seen her mother in such shape.

Sunday came. John went to Christmas services alone. "Sister Anne's not feeling well today," he announced, not knowing how to explain the situation.

Anne arose early on Monday, Christmas morning. After making coffee, she woke up John. "Let me sleep a little bit longer," he mumbled.

"John, I'm leaving here," she said simply. "I

want you to go with me but whether you do or not
I'm leaving."

John saw a look in her eyes. He got up and began
packing. "How many clothes are you taking? We
won't need much. Huh?"

"I'm taking enough clothes to go anywhere I want
and stay as long as I want ... because I don't know if
I'm coming back."

The sound of her voice made John know that something was seriously wrong. He wondered what could
he do.

They left, heading south. "Let's go to Texas and see
your folks," John suggested after they'd been on the
road several hours.

Anne nodded. It didn't make any difference to her,
just as long as they left Virginia Beach behind.

Three days later, they arrived in Corpus Christi
visiting briefly with her folks and checking into a
motel. Each day, they swam in a heated pool and
sweated in a sauna — but above all — they relaxed.
Anne's taunt emotions eased.

After a week, Anne mentioned the church's New
Year's service. "You really ought to think about
flying back."

"I'm not leaving you," he replied.

Anne went so far as to make airline reservations
for John, but he canceled them. "I won't leave you
here alone," he said softly.

One day they sat poolside talking about their situation. "It's like being on the road in the old days," Anne
reminded him.

"Yeah," he agreed. "You know, I was thinking about
putting Robin in school out here and maybe doing

some meetings in Texas for a while."

"That's an idea," Anne replied.

A few days went by. They made plans to speak in several cities in Texas and Oklahoma. Only once did John call back to Virginia Beach.

Speculation and fear arose at Rock Church over their absence. No one seemed to know why they'd left so abruptly. Was God going to take them away now? Would they ever come back? Many at Rock Church prayed for them.

16

"When Is Rock Church Gonna Quit Growing?"

Several weeks passed. Anne's frayed nerves and tired body slowly mended. Healing came gradually. "Did you realize I was leaving you, the church and everything a couple weeks ago?" Anne asked one afternoon.

He nodded. "I knew it."

"I didn't realize how bad my nerves were," she admitted. "I was so frustrated and tired I couldn't see it."

John reached for her hand. "I realized as never before that you were totally dependent on me," he said.

She smiled.

"Twelve years ago God used your strength to help turn me around," he continued. "Now it was time for me to do the same for you."

She nodded, patting his hand. "When I look back now at the situation, I can see the devil was trying to destroy me," she suggested. "It was such an ordeal."

"Yeah — it makes me think the Lord is really going to do something big, because the attack would have hurt us, and then the church."

"You're right."

"Let's go home," she suddenly enthused.

"I was waiting for you to say that," he shouted.

When they returned to Virginia Beach, their mailbox plus their desks were piled high with letters of appreciation and gratitude. It seemed like every person who'd ever attended Rock Church wrote a personal letter expressing their love for what the Gimenezes had done in their lives. In adjoining offices, John and Anne wept and laughed over the mail. It was good to be back.

A new challenge immediately lay before them. Fred Teagle, the elder in charge of finances, approached John shortly after he'd returned. "A committee from the Presbyterian Church has approached us asking if we'd be interested in swapping some of our acreage for their property," he wondered.

"We would indeed," John greeted the question.

The Kempsville Presbyterian Church located across a side street had mushroomed in recent years. David Anderson, the church's pastor, often joked with John saying, "We're getting your overflow. People come here when they can't find a seat at your place."

Several elders at Rock Church had thoughts about the Presbyterian land. "I think it's going to be ours one day," they mentioned from time to time.

"Don't say too much about that," John always responded, "I don't want to make enemies with those folks."

But the miracle had truly happened. Rock Church would be able to trade some of its acreage for the Presbyterian Church land, then sell off the remainder for a neat profit. The extra space was desperately needed for the mushrooming church. The added eight and a half acres was gladly received.

Many times the Gimenezes prayed over the future direction of Rock Church. They were astounded at the miracles of God — property and building's worth $5 million debt-free, the Bible Institute, Rock Christian Academy, the affiliate churches, the children's home in India, the church-supported missionaries, the nationwide television ministry. Where would it all end? There seemed so much to do.

Once during a public hearing over the church's girls' home which the City of Kempsville had ordered closed, a frustrated woman asked that same question. "You people promised us you'd just be a neighborhood church when you moved here," she said hotly. "You're not a neighborhood church ... in fact, you're not a national church. You're a *worldwide* church. But what I want to know is when is Rock Church gonna quit growing?"

The room was quiet for a moment. Then a lone voice from another corner of the room suggested, "Why don't you ask God, lady?"

Demos Shakarian, president/founder of the Full Gospel Businessmen, had been to Rock Church shortly after the first building was dedicated. He was thrilled at God's blessings then, but on his initial visit to the round building, he was overjoyed.

"I thought the other place was great," he gushed, "but this sanctuary is just mind-boggling."

The crowd shouted and applauded.

John and Anne came forward to share the pulpit with the respected white-haired leader. "This is a tribute to what God can do in the lives of people who simply yield," Demos smiled, putting his arms around the Gimenezes and giving them both an affectionate hug. "I love your pastors."

People cheered.

Everyone realized — as did the Gimenezes — the truth of Demos Shakarian's words. It all agreed with a prophecy that Pastor Emanuel Canistracci had given just three brief years before.

"And surely the Lord shall use thee and make thy lives as a display of what a husband and wife can do together in the Kingdom of God – out of love and respect, and preferring each other and each other's ministry – with no competition or rivalry. Surely the Lord hath raised thee up as an example of what He shall do in these last days..."